CANINE BOOT CAMP

Basic Training for the Dog You Love

Rick Caran

Adams Media
Avon, Massachusetts

Published by
Adams Media, an F+W Publications Company
57 Littlefield Street, Avon, MA 02322. U.S.A.
www.adamsmedia.com

ISBN 10: 1-59869-090-6
ISBN 13: 978-1-59869-090-3

Printed in Canada.

J I H G F E D C B A

Library of Congress Cataloging-in-Publication Data
available from publisher

This publication is designed to provide accurate and authoritative information
with regard to the subject matter covered. It is sold with the understanding that
the publisher is not engaged in rendering legal, accounting, or other professional
advice. If legal advice or other expert assistance is required, the services of a
competent professional person should be sought.
—From a *Declaration of Principles* jointly adopted by a Committee of the
American Bar Association and a Committee of Publishers and Associations

Many of the designations used by manufacturers and sellers to distinguish their
product are claimed as trademarks. Where those designations appear in this book
and Adams Media was aware of a trademark claim, the designations have been
printed with initial capital letters.

Contains portions of material adapted and abridged from *The Everything*® *Dog Book*
by Carlo DeVito and Amy Ammen, ©1999, F+W Publications, Inc.; *The Everything*®
Puppy Book by Carlo DeVito and Amy Ammen ©2002, F+W Publications, Inc.; *The
Everything*® *Dog Training and Tricks Book* by Gerilyn J. Bielakiewicz, ©2003, F+W
Publications, Inc.; and *The Everything*® *Dog Health Book* by Kim Campbell Thornton
and Debra Eldredge, D.V.M., ©2005, F+W Publications, Inc.

This book is available at quantity discounts for bulk purchases.
For information, please call 1-800-289-0963.

CONTENTS

Introduction

Hamlet was a treasured member of my family, from the beginning of time, or so it seemed to me as an eight-year-old. He was a gentle giant of a Great Dane, who I would lie next to or right on top of, and hang out with. My four brothers and I were told of how Hamlet once stopped a baby carriage containing one of us from rolling down a hilly street when my mom turned away for a moment. And then there was the time when I was two and had "disappeared." Hamlet seemed to understand what the frantic search was about and sniffed me out in the laundry closet taking a nap. He barked to alert the family that I had been found—a scene right out of Lassie.

I never considered training him. Me, an 85-pound, nine-year-old, train this 190-pound gentle giant? He seemed to have natural wisdom, knew what to do, and certainly seemed to know right from wrong. Hamlet was like my third parent; he took care of us.

Then Skippy came along when I was nine. Skippy was a mutt, a little black and white stray. But, best of all, Skippy was mine. It was the old story: My folks said, "You can keep this dog, *if* you care for it." Because he was mine, the very first living creature that was all mine, I felt the need and responsibility to be there for him. I was all he had.

Hamlet seemed to be as attached to this little scruffy pup as I was and Skippy adored him and followed him everywhere. While Hamlet was princely, Skippy was a court jester. He made me laugh all the time. I learned my very first lesson about training dogs from Skippy. I noticed that he felt good when I was smiling and he quite obviously went through antics to get me to smile. He was aware of my emotions. When I was sad, he was sad. When I was scared, he would comfort me. But mostly, when I was happy, he was happy— very happy! It was my first lesson in the value of positive reinforcement. I realized that you can accomplish so much more with a smile than you can with anger.

I didn't think of it as training. I was just having fun, teaching him a few tricks. The more I taught him, the smarter he became, or so it seemed. He absorbed every lesson and begged for more. There was a communication that developed with this little pup that amazed me. It was in the eyes—a knowing, understanding, and loving look.

I began training Skippy a little every day. Then, to my amazement, I noticed that Hamlet, who was always there, started imitating some of the things I was teaching Skippy. I started including him in the lessons. At eleven years old, he was slowing down a bit, but this seemed to perk him up. He was as excited as Skippy at training time. I learned that you *can* teach old dogs new tricks. Maybe not as many or as fast, but it can be done.

I don't know if they had much in the way of dog training manuals in the 1950s, but *Canine Boot Camp* reflects the self-taught methods I discovered as a boy, and gets to the heart of it more directly. This book is more than just a dog training manual; it's a dog training philosophy, stressing the use of positive reinforcement, rather than punishment to achieve desired results. It discusses many aspects of the canine/human relationship, including the characteristics of various breeds, as well as how to discover and deal with the personality and ability of your own dog, and much, much more.

What do a good boot camp drill instructor and a good dog trainer have in common? They both strive to produce good citizens through conditioning, practice, repetition, education, and discipline, delivered with love. Love? Yes, even the crustiest drill sergeants want to prepare their trainees for the world, as they would their own children.

We share our homes, our lives, and our love with these wonderful canine creatures; why not, using the right training methods, develop your dog into one that's a pleasure to be with.

—Rick Caran

CHAPTER 1

Enlistment: What Is Your Dog Like?

Taking a moment to get an idea of "who" your dog is can help you design a training program that will be effective in teaching him to fit in with your family. Finding out how your dog responds to distractions and whether toys or games motivate him may be helpful in putting together a basic training program that is easy to implement.

How Well Do You Know Your Recruit?

Breaking your training sessions down into small steps, finding out what motivates your dog, and finding out where your dog is most distracted will help you know where to start. Below are some questions you might want to ask yourself before you begin your training program.

- Is he energetic or laid back? A maniac retriever or a couch potato?
- Does he do something that you've always meant to put on cue but didn't know how to?
- Is his attention span short or long? How does he respond amid distractions?

1

- What is his favorite treat or toy?
- Does he give up easily or does he persist until he gets the job done?

Understanding your dog's personality and learning style is essential to enjoyably and successfully teaching him tricks or anything else. Combining an energetic dog with a fast-moving and flashy trick is exciting and invigorating not only for the dog, but also for your audience. Knowing your dog includes knowing what motivates him. Finding just the right kind of treat, toy, or game will help your dog associate training with fun and help your training program be a success.

Energy Level

Some dogs are couch potatoes; others run circles around us all day. Differences in breed, temperament, and personality all come into play when designing a successful training program. Living with your dog makes you the expert when it comes to knowing the ins and outs of her personality and just what will work for her. Paying attention to how active your dog is can help you learn about her personality and help you train and teach.

Highly Active

Active dogs love active training because they make the most of natural behaviors, such as spinning, jumping, barking, and pawing. When dogs have this much energy, take advantage of their abilities and teach appropriate tricks and training regiments.

However, high-energy dogs get overstimulated easily, and do best in short, concise training sessions with clear goals in mind. If you don't push high-energy dogs to work for long periods, they will fall in love with learning.

Less Active

Lower-energy dogs may be harder to get moving until they figure out what you want them to do. These dogs are thinkers, and they like to know where you're going with all this. Go slowly with your dog. Try to keep your sessions short, because such dogs often bore easily and hate repeating things too many times in a row. Training before a meal (using unique treats as rewards) often perks them up and lets you get a good session in.

Medium-energy dogs are the easiest to work with because they allow you to make a lot of mistakes and be less organized. They don't mind repeating things over and over, and they are patient with you when you make mistakes or haven't planned out what you are trying to teach. Dogs with moderate energy levels are laid back and fun, turning their energy on like a rocket booster when they need to, but generally going along with whatever you're doing.

Personality

Ask yourself some questions about your dog's personality traits to discover where to begin your training program. It can save a lot of time if you start training your dog in an environment that isn't so distracting that he can't pay attention. An outgoing dog will love tricks that he can perform in a crowd, while a wallflower may prefer performing at a bit of a distance. Teaching your dog where he is most relaxed and least distracted, or worried, will help him be successful.

Social Temperament

A dog that is easily distracted by her friendliness around people will benefit from training sessions that start somewhere quiet, then quickly move on to involve the distractions she finds hard to resist. Training your dog to perform around distractions from the start is one way to ensure that her performance will not fall apart in public.

Shy dogs, on the other hand, may resist training in public until they are more confident. With this type of dog, practice in the most comfortable environment possible, and then gradually integrate distractions with familiar people. The ultimate goal is to incorporate strangers and new places so that your dog can perform anywhere.

Special Talents and Interests

Depending on a dog's breed characteristics, he will often display a natural talent for certain tricks or training. For instance, Labrador and Golden retrievers often excel at tricks that involve having things in their mouths, like Put Away Your Toys or Go Fetch Me a Coke from the Refrigerator. Herding breeds might prefer to learn directional tricks like spinning to the left or right. A small dog that stands on its hind legs a lot may be a great candidate to learn Sit Up and Beg or Dance. A large-breed dog may be perfect for Play Dead, especially if he is of the low-energy mindset.

Dogs are amazing creatures, and they are so willing to be with us and please us that they will put up with a lot so long as they are getting attention. With enough patience and practice, and the right training tools, you can teach your dog to do just about anything!

Keep Safety in Mind

Keep your dog's safety in mind while you are training, and pay attention to its physical limitations. For larger breeds like Great Danes and Saint Bernards, you may not want to do tricks that involve jumping, since the impact of landing is not good for joints.

⊕ ABOUT FACE!

Jumping can be harmful to long-bodied dogs, as they can injure their spines. Pay attention to your dog's weight, also, since extra pounds can lead to injuries and joint problems later in life. If you respect your dog's physical limitations, he will amaze you with his willingness to try what you ask.

A dog cannot tell you outright if something is uncomfortable, so do your best to read his body language and go slowly. As often as possible, perform on a soft surface like a rug, grass, or sand, especially for tricks involving jumping, spinning, or rolling. Being mindful of your environment will minimize injuries and make your dog more comfortable.

What Motivates Your Pooch?

Learning what your dog likes as rewards is crucial to being a successful dog trainer. Many people are surprised to learn that dog cookies and dry dog food just don't cut it. Be creative in what you offer your dog as rewards, and keep the pieces tiny if it's food. Even a Great Dane shouldn't get a treat larger than ¼ inch. Keeping the treats tiny will ensure that you'll be able to train for a longer period of time, because your dog won't get full too fast. It will also help you not to add too many calories to his daily requirement. Think about cutting his daily ration back a bit if you've had an extra-long training session.

The reward is your dog's paycheck for playing this training game with you. It has to be something he's willing to work for, not simply something you want him to have. Some people have hang-ups about using food to train dogs because it cheapens their bond with the dog. They believe the dog should perform out of respect or love for them. Nonsense. Using food to train your dog is a way to get where you want to go. Training a dog with what he wants as a reward is both respectful to his doggy-ness and effective in the interest of time and resources.

Dogs don't perform out of love; their behavior or misbehavior has nothing to do with their love for us. Even dogs that chew the couch and bite the postman love their owners. But if you want that postman-biter to like the postman, you'll probably have to use a reward that the dog likes a little more than a pat on the head.

Dogs are motivated by and will work for food, just like people work for money. We all need money to pay our bills and live our lives; dogs need food to live and enjoy theirs. Many dogs eat out of a bowl once or twice a day for free. Why not take that food and train them to behave in a way that is acceptable to you? Once a dog is hooked on training and you have a good bond with her, you can use other rewards to reinforce good or appropriate behavior. Here are some yummy ideas for treats:

- Boiled chicken
- Boiled hamburger
- Popcorn
- Tortellini or other types of pasta (cooked)
- Bread (bagel pieces work great)
- Carrots
- Bananas
- Dried fruit
- Cheerios or other types of cereal
- Freeze-dried liver (found in pet stores and supply catalogs)
- Hot dogs (cooked)

To prevent your dog from getting diarrhea, don't give too much of any one thing. As your dog starts to like the training game, mix in less desirable treats (like dog food) with the yummy stuff so that he never knows what he is getting. Random reinforcement will keep him more interested in the game and let you accomplish more in each training session.

Other Rewards

Most of the time we use a food reward in training because it is quick and easy. In beginner classes especially, students use treats because there is a lot to accomplish in only one hour a week. If yours is a dog that goes nuts over tennis balls or stuffed toys, or he likes Frisbees or chasing a flashlight beam, use these rewards paired with the click.

Toys and games are a whole different category of rewards that may be exciting to your dog. If you find your dog likes games and toys, make your training sessions even more exciting by mixing them in with food rewards. Some sessions could be all food rewards or all toys and games, or you can mix it up and see what elicits the best response.

✪ ABOUT FACE!

As with anything in life, there is truth to the phrase "too much of a good thing." Rewards, especially food, can lose the name "treat" if you give them to your dog for everything he does. Use moderation—it encourages your dog to get the treat through good behavior!

When using toys as a reward, the key is to make the play part brief and fun. The game might last five to ten seconds, and then the toy gets hidden and you get back to work. That way the reward doesn't distract the dog from the lesson. Here are some ideas for nonfood rewards:

- A short game of fetch
- A short game of tug
- A short game of catch
- Hide a toy and go find it together
- Toss a Frisbee

- Chase a stream of bubbles
- Lots of happy praise and baby talk
- Vigorous petting and happy talk
- Flashlight tag (have your dog chase the light beam)
- A stuffed dog toy
- A stuffed dog toy that makes noise
- A squeaky toy

Dogs are affectionate animals, and any time you spend praising them and showering them with attention is time well spent. Chances are, you'll get as much from the affection and exercise as they do!

Help Your Dog Like Other Rewards

Some dogs love toys and will happily work for a toss of the ball at least part of the time. Dogs who are not as crazy for toys can learn to like them if you work at it. It is worth the effort on your part to get the dog interested in varied rewards, because the more he finds rewarding the easier it will be for you and the more effective your sessions will be. Here's how to get started:

1. Hold your dog on a leash and tease him with a toy.
2. Throw the toy out of range and ignore his struggle toward it, but don't let him get it.
3. Use a helper to make the toy more exciting if necessary.
4. Wait patiently until the dog looks away from the toy and back at you.

5. Mark that moment with a click and allow him to go play with the toy as the reward.
6. If he doesn't turn away from the toy in about thirty seconds, slowly back up to increase the distance between the dog and the toy. Click and release him to get the toy when your dog looks back at you.
7. Repeat this with different toys and allow the dog to go play with the helper every once in a while.
8. The play part of the reward is brief, about ten seconds.

This exercise should help you rev up a dog that is only mildly interested in toys. Warming him up this way is a great way to start a training session—it helps the dog realize that it's time to work.

Exciting rewards are critical to an effective program. If your dog isn't turning himself inside out for the reward, find something he likes better. Don't worry if you just can't get your dog interested in toys; there is no crime in using food in training. Remember, dogs love to eat, so why not combine eating and training?

Reward or Bribe?

Using food to teach your dog to perform tricks is simple, fun, and effective. One problem many people complain about, however, is that in the absence of food the dog won't perform the behavior. That just means that you aren't there yet. If you use food correctly, you won't need to use it to get the dog to perform the trick; it will come after the trick has been performed. This is the critical difference between a reward and a bribe.

A bribe is something that causes a behavior to happen by enticing the dog. For example, your dog is out in the yard and won't come in, so you shake a box of cookies to bribe him in. This isn't really a bad thing, but it isn't training either. Bribing can have its benefits, however, when you are in a hurry and out of options.

A reward, on the other hand, is something that occurs only after a behavior happens. A reward reinforces the likelihood that the behavior will happen again. For instance, you call your dog at the park and he comes to you; you offer a treat and release him back to play again. A rewarded dog is far more likely to come to you the next time you call than is a dog that is put back on leash and put in the car to go home. There are two types of rewards at work here: the food reward, which reinforced the dog for performing the behavior of coming back to his owner; and the consequence for coming back, which was that he got to go play again.

If you know your dog well—his energy level, personality, special talents, limitations, and motivations—you will be able to choose tricks that make both of you shine. Spend some time with your dog over the next few days and make notes on each of these categories. You may be surprised to learn how many things you assumed he would like that he actually doesn't. Adjusting your teaching style and training sessions can have a profound impact on the success of your training program.

Exercise First; Training Will Follow

Exercise is a crucial element in any training program, and without it, no real learning will occur. A dog without enough exercise is like a child without recess. What adult would like to teach a math lesson to a classroom full of six-year-old boys who haven't been outside to play all day? Without exercise, your dog will be hard to teach because he can't be still long enough to pay attention.

Dogs vary in their exercise requirements, but all need at least thirty minutes of running, playing, and interaction with you each day. The amount and type of exercise is dependent upon your dog's overall energy level. A Border collie or active young Lab will need one to two hours of flat-out running and active play, while a couch potato Pekingese may need only a thirty-minute romp. Yet every dog is different, regardless of the breed and its stereotype. Ultimately, the amount of exercise your dog needs is whatever it takes to make her tired enough to be able to exist in your home as a calm, relaxed member of the family. Following are some clues that your dog isn't getting enough exercise:

- She paces from room to room in the house.
- She hardly ever lies down, even when everyone else is relaxed.
- She whines excessively for no apparent reason.
- She barks excessively, sometimes over nothing.
- She digs, destroys, and chews everything in sight.
- She never stops jumping when there are people around.
- She runs away every chance she gets.
- She runs along the fence using any excuse to bark at passersby.

If your dog exhibits some or all of these symptoms, she could probably use more exercise and mental stimulation. Most people don't realize that leaving their dogs in the backyard for hours at a time is not a good way to burn off energy and not nearly enough exercise to make for a relaxed family pet. Most dogs, when left to their own devices, don't do anything but bark or dig or lay around.

⊙ ABOUT FACE

Giving your dog adequate exercise is a great way to spend time together—and an opportunity to get exercise yourself! Take a long walk with your recruit, or play some ball for a while every day. You'll be surprised how convenient it is!

If you are going to use your yard as a way to exercise your dog, you will need to go out with her and play games to burn off even one-tenth of the energy she's got bottled up. Inviting neighbor dogs over to play, if your dog gets along with them, might be another option. All-out running, chasing, and wrestling is what a dog needs to do in order to be tired enough to be a good pet.

Work Out Together

For dog owners with an active lifestyle, there are lots of ways a healthy active dog can burn off energy while accompanying you. Jogging, mountain biking, and Rollerblading are excellent ways to exercise dogs with boundless energy. Just make sure that you start off slowly and gradually build the distance. Also, pay attention to your dog's feet, checking them frequently for cuts and scrapes. Try to have him run on a variety of surfaces, since pavement is hard on a dog's joints and bones. Be aware of especially hot surfaces in summer or cold surfaces in the winter.

Dogs that participate in such activities should be at least one year old and recently checked by their veterinarian for potential health problems. (Just as it can with people, vigorous exercise can exacerbate certain bone and joint disorders.) A word of caution-- dogs love to be with their humans and may not show discomfort or pain. Go slowly at first and be aware of your dog's condition. A fit dog is happier, and you will find that he is more focused on what- ever activity you are enjoying together, and he will be more likely to do it longer and without injury.

Dog Sports and Activities

The reason we get dogs in the first place is to enjoy their com- pany and share them with other people. Depending on your dog's personality and activity level, you may consider participating with your dog in any of a great variety of dog sports or activities. Enroll- ing your dog in an agility class might be an excellent way to intro- duce both of you to something new while maintaining a good level of fitness. Agility is an obstacle course for dogs involving things to climb over, around, and through, as well as hurdles to jump over. The course is timed and dependent on you being able to success- fully lead your dog through a maze of obstacles to the finish.

If you would like to be an active participant in your dog's exer- cise program, you will find that there are many canine sports that require you to be almost as fit as your dog. From fly ball to track- ing to search and rescue, the possibilities are endless. If your style is quieter, you may consider a visiting-therapy dog program that allows you to go and visit a hospital or nursing home on a weekly or monthly basis. This is an excellent way to meet other dog owners and keep your dog's obedience skills sharp, because you will be using them constantly.

If you have free time and financial resources, you may consider becoming part of the growing search and rescue dog teams that look for missing people locally and nationally. No matter what your interest, there is a dog sport that you and your pup will both enjoy.

Games Dogs Play

Dog games are a great way to boost his interest in learning new things and strengthen your bond with him at the same time. Regardless of the game, the true objective is to make sure you both have fun. Keep the rules simple and easy to follow, and play often. Involve as many people in the family as you can, and see how much fun it can be to learn new ways of interacting together. Consider any of the following activities and games:

Play Fetch—a great way to tire out a tireless retriever. Use a tennis racquet to hit the ball that much further for all-out sprints.

Go swimming—another great way to exercise a very active dog. Combine it with some retrieving for a really exhausting workout.

Play hide-and-seek—an indoor rainy-day game may provide some dogs with enough activity to let them sleep the rest of the day. Also use this game to perk up your dog's recall and teach him that coming to you is always the best option.

Hide your dog's toys—he'll learn to use his nose to track things down *and* bring them back to you.

Learn a new trick—practice until it's perfect, then show off to your friends and family.

Practice Pavlov—set up a treat-dispensing toy, and show your dog how to interact with it until it pays off.

Whatever you do, be sure you are having a blast! Keep it fun, and keep the pace fast and interesting; you will see your dog perk up at the mere mention of playtime with you.

Provide the Right Foundation for Learning

Mental stimulation is the second-most overlooked need of problem dogs. Learning new things and solving problems make life interesting and give smart dogs something to do—and keeps them out of trouble, too! All dogs, regardless of breed or energy level, are intelligent and interactive creatures that love new experiences.

Dogs that are tied outside, constantly frustrated, and emotionally neglected may start off friendly and welcoming, but eventually become aggressive and wary of strangers. They have nothing to do, nothing to think about, and are absolutely bored. Dogs like this, even early in their adult lives (two to three years old), are hard to train. They aren't stupid or uncooperative, just blank. They simply do not know how to learn.

Lack of early stimulation and training makes it more difficult to teach any animal at a later date, because he has no basis for and doesn't quite know what to make of the attention. It is possible to teach these dogs, but it takes patience, repetition, and practice. The training methods and tools described in the succeeding chapters will help you teach your dog anything you care to take the time to teach.

Teach Your Dog to Think

The training methods described in this book teach your dog how to think and solve problems, which is important for any dog. The techniques are commonly referred to as "clicker training," and are based in proven scientific theory. The rules and guidelines will show you how to use this method to teach your dog anything physically possible. It is so exciting to see a dog grasp the concept of what you are trying to accomplish, and respond so well without needing any corrections!

All puppies should attend a well-run puppy kindergarten class that teaches you how to teach your dog the basic commands (Sit, Down, Stay, Come), how to walk without pulling, and to come when called. The class should also offer a playtime for dogs in the eight- to eighteen-week range, and should be staff-supervised so everyone has a good experience. It is crucial to the normal social development of your dog that she gets to play with other puppies and safe, well-socialized adult dogs on a regular basis. The more good experiences your young puppy has the easier it will be to teach her anything later in life.

The following is a list of qualities to look for in your dog-training school:

- A limited class size with an instructor/assistant-to-student ratio of 1:6 is ideal.
- The age range of the puppies accepted should be no older than eighteen weeks.
- Handouts or homework sheets to explain exercises are important so that lessons can be shared among family members.
- The whole family should be welcome to attend. (If you include your children, make sure you bring along another adult to supervise them while you focus on training the dog.)
- All training methods should be positively based, ideally clicker training.
- Demonstrations should be given with untrained dogs to show the progression of exercises.
- Volunteers or assistants who help with the management of the class should be available to ensure that you get the help you need.

The best judge of a good puppy kindergarten, or any obedience class for that matter, is you. Ask if you can observe a class before signing up your puppy. Make sure the methods taught are kind and gentle, and that the puppies seem to be getting it. Go on your gut instinct—if you like the instructor and she seems like a person you can learn from, sign up. Train your dog; it's the nicest way to say you love him!

Practice and Consistency Is the Key

As with anything in which you want to excel, the more you practice the better at it you will become. All training is a learned skill; the more you work with your dog, the more effective you'll be as a trainer and as a team. For example, the beginning trainer is notoriously stingy with rewards, and her timing needs some work. Through lots of practice, you will find and develop your own training style, discovering what works for you and expanding upon it.

Tons of resources are available, through books and online, that will tell you everything you'll ever want to know about behavior and training. Search for obedience classes in your area and keep at it. Remember that your dog and you are going to be together for a very long time, if you're lucky maybe even ten to twelve years or longer. Time spent teaching her how to learn will benefit both of you for years to come. Start your dog on the road to higher learning today!

CHAPTER 2

Different Types of Basic Training

Despite the rigorous training and fierce determination, dog training has become kinder and gentler to both the dog and the owner. No longer is it necessary to use brute force or intimidation to force a dog to comply in its first months as your recruit. Training any animal is about opening lines of communication and learning a common language. Clicker training isn't a gimmick or the latest fad; it is a scientifically based technique that utilizes the positive principles of operant conditioning.

The Kindness Revolution in Dog Training

Use clicker training to teach your dog what you expect of him; it's an intelligent and time-saving endeavor. Positive reinforcement through the use of treats and a clicker will help you teach your dog to think. The old style of training—making the dog "obey"—is not only outdated, it also does not evolve his problem-solving skills or intelligence.

Training your dog with treats and a clicker is the fastest, most reliable way to train your dog and have fun while you are doing it. There is no need to coerce, push, or shove to get what you want; once your dog knows how to learn, you will have a willing partner and a better overall relationship. Hundreds of families have learned to train their dogs with a clicker and treats and have enjoyed the learning process so much that they have come back again and again for more advanced classes.

The application of clicker training to dogs is pure genius; it simplifies and speeds up the process of learning for dogs and owners alike. Handlers of any age or size can learn the principles of clicker training, and since it is not dependent on corrections or physical manipulation, the size, strength, and stamina of the handler doesn't matter.

Getting Started with a Clicker

The clicker is a small plastic box with a metal tab that makes a clicking sound when you push down with your thumb. The sound of the click is paired with a food reward by clicking the clicker and giving the dog a treat. After a few repetitions, the dog learns to associate the sound of the clicker with a food reward.

Why It Works

The click marks the desired behavior to identify for the dog which behavior earned the reward. Because the food is removed by a step—you click first and then treat—you will find that your dog will work for the sound of the click rather than just a food reward. By pairing the clicker with a food reward, we have created a powerful way to communicate to our dogs what behaviors are rewardable. This comes in handy, especially with a very active dog, because it gives you a way to specify to the dog exactly which of the behaviors earned the reward.

Think of the click as a snapshot of what the dog is doing at the exact moment he is doing it. The click clearly identifies for the dog which behavior is being rewarded. Not only does this make it easier for the dog to understand what he is doing right, but it also gets him excited about the learning process since it gives him the responsibility for making the click happen.

The Clicker As an Event Marker

The sound of the click is unique, like nothing that the dog has ever heard, which is part of the key to its success. People often ask about using their voices instead of the clicker to mark the behavior they are looking for. In the initial stages of training your voice is not a good event marker because you talk to your dog all the time, so your voice lacks the startling effect that the clicker invokes.

 ABOUT FACE!

The process of shaping is what clicker training is all about. Shaping is useful in all types of training, but it is crucial in teaching tricks. Shaping behavior helps the dog learn how to think about what they did to earn the reward. By not helping him or physically manipulating his body, you help your dog learn faster and more permanently by trial and error.

The clicker's uniqueness reaches the part of the brain that is also responsible for the fight-or-flight response. In short, it really captures the dog's attention.

Shaping

Shaping behavior means breaking it down into steps that progress toward an end goal. Shaping is not a rigid list of steps, but rather a general guide to get from point A to point B with lots of room for variation, intuition, rapid progress (skipping steps), or reviewing if the steps are too big.

Prompted and Free Shaping

Shaping can be either prompted, using a food lure or target, or free shaped. Free shaping requires waiting for the dog to offer desired actions on his own, then rewarding him with a treat in order to capture the small steps of behavior that lead toward the end goal. Each trick you learn here will be broken down into its component parts. You can then embellish upon those steps if your dog needs things broken down further.

Keep notes on each trick you teach, and whether your dog is catching on to the components as presented or needs more explicit direction. You will find that detailed notes make it easy to pick up where you left off, and your training sessions will be more productive overall. You will reach your goals faster if you have a plan.

For behaviors that involve natural talents or unusual behaviors, free shaping is the way to go. Because the dog is fully in charge of which behaviors she is offering, she will often learn faster (in some situations) and retain more than when you prompt her behavior with a lure or target. Free shaping can be time-consuming, however, since it depends upon the dog offering behavior, and it requires patience on the handler's part.

Working Through a Shaping Plan

Teaching a dog that likes to jump on guests to Sit instead is a lot more complicated than teaching just a Sit/Stay. The reason for this is due to all the distractions and variables during any given greeting. Though a dog may be able to Sit when there are no distractions, this doesn't mean he'll be able to Sit when a kid with a hot dog approaches him or when he sees his favorite person. Dogs need to be taught how to Sit and Stay around gradually more stimulating distractions; they don't automatically generalize their behavior to all environments.

Teaching your dog to Sit instead of jumping requires that you break sitting down into small steps that are easy for the dog to accomplish but at the same time introduce challenging distractions slowly so as to maintain the right behavior. The steps to teach Sit/Stay around distractions are as follows:

1. Teach your dog to Sit by luring her with a treat, then clicking and treating her when her bottom hits the floor.
2. Once your dog is performing this well, delay the click by counting to two before you click and treat. This is the beginning of a mini-Stay.
3. Increase the amount of seconds between the time your dog sits and the click and treat until your dog is holding the Sit behavior for ten seconds at a time.
4. Once your dog can hold the Sit for ten seconds between clicks and treats, go ahead and verbally label the behavior Stay and include a hand signal if desired.

5. Help your dog generalize this behavior by going somewhere new or adding in distractions. You may have to lower your standards and start from the beginning until your dog learns to block out the distractions and pay attention to you instead.

6. Add in people approaching your dog from the side and not making eye contact.

7. Add in people approaching your dog from the front and looking at him.

8. Add in people petting her or talking to her.

9. Continue to change the variables until your dog will hold the Sit/Stay position regardless of the distraction.

10. As your dog starts to be able to handle the distractions and works longer and more consistently, wean her off the clicker and treats so that she will perform the behavior for the reward of being able to greet the person.

By implementing this shaping plan, you can teach your dog to sit regardless of what is happening in the environment, or who she is greeting.

A less formal way to teach the same thing is listed on the following page; you might try both shaping plans to see which one is more suited to your training style. The following shaping plan does not help the dog by luring him with a treat when he makes the wrong decision. Instead, this shaping sequence lets the dog make choices. You click only those choices that lead toward the goal of sitting and staying.

1. Start off by clicking and treating the dog for any behavior except jumping (standing, sitting, lying down, walking around) for the first minute.
2. The second minute choose something specific and click and treat him every time he offers it. You'll want to pick something easy, like standing still for one second or walking without whining, so that he can easily succeed.
3. If you have an active dog that offers a lot of behaviors, you might want to limit his options by putting him on a leash and stepping on it so that jumping is not an option.
4. Continue working with the dog in short sessions until he starts to visibly startle at the sound of the click and holds the position for a second.
5. Next, withhold the click for a while and see what happens; most dogs will Sit out of confusion and boredom, and you can click and treat that.
6. As soon as the dog Sits (on his own without being prompted), click and treat.
7. Repeat this over and over and gradually increase the amount of seconds the dog has to hold the Sit for a click and treat, until you have the dog holding the Sit for a reasonable amount of time.
8. You can continue on this way to polish the Sit to greet visitors in any way you wish.

Regardless of which shaping plan you choose, you will see that there are times when things will go fast and smoothly, and you may even skip steps or make great leaps in your shaping plan. Other times you will come to a standstill as your dog gets muddled and confused about what he's supposed to do. You will need to re-evaluate your plan and break it down into further steps or help him out in some way. Learning how to shape behavior will make you a better overall dog trainer and make training your dog more fun.

Using Lures in Training

A lure is a piece of food used to elicit behavior. Its goal is to help the dog get into the right position in order to earn the click and treat. In beginning your career as a dog trainer it is often frustrating and time consuming to wait for your dog to offer the right behavior, so the use of a food lure gets things going. The problem with food lures is that unless they are faded relatively quickly, the dog (and humans) become dependent upon them in order to perform the behavior. If lures are not faded, you will not have a trained dog that can perform behaviors on cue; you will have a trained dog that follows food.

As a general rule, lure the dog six times in a row. On the seventh repetition, do all the same motions with your body, but without the food lure in your hand. If the dog performs the behavior correctly, click and treat. If he doesn't perform the behavior correctly, go back and lure him six more times and try it again. This mini-drilling session trains the dog on how to perform the correct behavior, and it lets you see if he understands what he's being clicked for.

Your goal with using a food lure is to help the dog into position six times in a row; then, on the seventh repetition, try hiding the lure to see if the dog starts to offer the behavior on her own. When you take the lure out of your hand, you can start fading it gradually by putting it on a nearby table and running to get it after the click. The dog knows it's there and is excited about it but is not dependent on you waving it around to get her into the right position.

Using this method to wean your dog off of lures means that you get the dog to perform the behavior, click, and then run to get the treat. Doing this exercise will help your dog to learn that she is working for the click, and that the treat is an afterthought.

Targeting

Targeting is a form of luring, but it removes the treat by a step. It involves teaching the dog to touch his nose to an object. You might use this tool in order to move your dog or have him interact with someone or something.

Anything can be used as a target, but the three main targets are your hand, a lid to a yogurt container, and a target stick. (You can buy a target stick online at *www.clickertraining.com* or make your own out of a short piece of dowel).

Hand Target

The goal with using targeting is to get the behavior started but then wean the dog off the target so that he is performing the behavior reliably without it. The same rules apply to weaning off the target as with weaning off the lure; use it to get the behavior started and then wean your dog off of it. To teach your dog to target your hand with his nose follow these steps.

1. Hold your hand palm up with a piece of food tucked under your thumb in the center of your palm. Click and treat your dog for sniffing your hand.
2. Keep the food in your hand for six repetitions and then take the food out and repeat, clicking the dog for touching his nose to your palm.
3. Have the dog follow your hand in all directions while you move around the room.
4. Involve a helper and have your dog target your hand and then your helper's hand for clicks and treats.
5. Label the behavior of touching his nose to your hand by saying Touch. (More on labeling follows.)
6. Try the trick in new places and with new people until your dog is fluent. Don't be afraid to go back to using food for a few repetitions if your dog falls apart around a new distraction.

Lid Target

On occasion, you may want your dog to move away from you to perform a behavior at a distance. In that case, it may be useful for you to teach your dog to target a yogurt lid with her nose. The steps for teaching your dog to target a lid are:

1. Put the lid in your hand and hold a treat in the center with your thumb.
2. When your dog noses at it, click and treat. Repeat for six repetitions.

3. Present the lid with no treat and click and treat for sniffing or nose bumping.
4. Label the behavior by saying Touch again just before your dog touches the lid.
5. Put the lid on the floor close by and repeat, clicking your dog at first for moving toward the lid and then for actually touching it with her nose.
6. Move the lid at varying distances until you can send her across the room to bump it with her nose for a click and treat.

Stick Target

Another variation of targeting involves using a stick as your target. The target stick acts like an extension of your arm and is useful in working with your dog at a little distance. The steps for teaching your dog to touch a target stick with his nose are as follows:

1. Put the end of the stick in the palm of your hand with a treat and click and treat your dog for sniffing or nudging at it with his nose.
2. Gradually work your hand up the stick and only click and treat your dog for touching his nose close to the end away from your hand.
3. Try putting the stick on the floor and only clicking and treating when your dog touches the ends.
4. Have your dog follow the stick as you walk with him until he's racing to catch the end of it for a click and treat.

Paw Targeting

There are times that you may want your dog to interact with an object with her paw instead of her nose. Teaching your dog to target with her paw may give you another tool that you can use to help her learn whatever trick you are teaching. The difference between teaching your dog to target with her paw instead of her nose involves paying attention to which body part is hitting the target.

1. Put your hand or lid out for the dog to see, but withhold the click until she steps near it. Because you have already taught your dog to target with her nose, she may offer only this behavior at first. Be patient and wait for paw action near the target.

2. Withhold the click to let your dog know that you want something other than a nose touch and see what happens.

3. Make it easy on your dog by moving the lid or your hand along the floor so that you can click her for moving toward it. An easy way to help your dog to get this behavior started is to put the lid at the base of the stairs and click her for stepping on or next to it.

4. When you withhold the click your dog may get frustrated, but don't be too quick to help right away; wait your dog out and see if she'll paw at the target or move toward it.

5. Practice a paw target separately from a nose target and be sure to have two distinctive cues for each one.

6. Frequent, short training sessions will help your dog figure out what you want faster than long, confusing ones.

For targeting to be useful, you must practice it often. The more experience your dog has with this method, the better it will serve you in your trick training.

Labeling Behavior

The major difference between clicker training and other types of training is that you don't label the behavior right away. The reason for this is that the early versions of the behavior are not what you want for the final behavior.

The first click for heeling, for instance, is a far cry from what the finished behavior will be. Saving the label until the dog is readily offering the behavior will ensure that the dog connects its behavior with what is being clicked, first.

 ABOUT FACE!

The label can come as a verbal cue or a hand signal or both, but should not be introduced until the dog is offering a decent version of it. If you label behavior too soon you will get a wide variety of responses from the dog. Wait until the behavior looks close to perfect before labeling it.

You can call each behavior anything you want, just be sure it is a simple one-syllable word as often as possible and try to be sure it doesn't sound too much like any other word you use with your dog. Dogs pick up a lot from your body language and the pitch of your voice but may have trouble distinguishing between similar sounding words, like *no* and *go* for instance.

Weaning off the Clicker and Treats

The clicker is a learning tool, a signal that identifies for the dog which behaviors will be rewarded. When the dog is performing the behavior on cue and reliably (with 100 percent accuracy), he is ready to be weaned off the clicker and treats. The click and treat always go together. You shouldn't click without treating because the value of the reward marker, the click, will become diluted and less meaningful to the dog.

One way to begin the weaning process is to have the dog repeat the behavior more than once before you click and treat. This gives the dog the idea that he must continue to perform the behavior until he hears his click. The worst thing you can do when you are weaning your dog off the clicker and treats is to do it cold turkey. Getting rid of rewards and affirmation that he is performing the behavior correctly all at once is too abrupt, and will result in a frustrated dog.

The key to weaning is going slowly, getting the dog to perform longer versions of the behavior, or performing it in more repetitions successfully. The weaning process may be a good time to start introducing nonfood rewards, such as the opportunity to go greet a guest after sitting, or being released to go play with other dogs after coming when called.

Treat Training

Most trainers want their puppies to obey out of love rather than because they were beaten or bribed. But is your love motivation enough? Not always, and you certainly don't want to end up disciplining your puppy for something that you can be teaching him pleasurably with something he's motivated for: a tasty treat.

There are basically three ways to use food:

- As a lure to get the puppy to perform a task
- As a reward for completing an already learned task
- As reinforcement for behaviors offered by the puppy (click and treat training)

Most people use treats and body language as a lure because it is the fastest way to entice the puppy to perform a task. But beware: there is a huge gap between following a lure and obeying a command. To bridge that gap, learn how to enforce your commands with your hands and leash. This will also prove invaluable if your puppy isn't interested in the treat because he's full or distracted.

The Last Word on Using Food

Eating is most dogs' greatest joy, a pleasure that you can use to help your dog learn appropriate manners and become a well-behaved member of your family. Regardless of a dog's preference for particular types of food, all dogs need to eat in order to survive. So, whether your dog is food oriented or not, every dog will work for food—you just may need to search a bit to find the right kind. What instructors love about clicker training is that it works for every dog.

Clicker training is successful because the emphasis is on the click not the treat. Once dogs figure out the game, they love it and will gladly work regardless of how they feel about food. If you have a finicky fellow, try diversifying what you use as the reward and cutting back a little on his daily meal.

For dogs that like to eat, you may have the opposite problem: too many calories. Clicker training uses a lot of food rewards, but that doesn't mean you'll have a fat dog. The size of the rewards should be tiny, ¼ of an inch or less, and can even consist of the dog's meals. If you have a particularly long training session, you can feed less food at the next meal or actually use the meal to train. The length of your sessions should be five to ten minutes maximum, so your dog is not going to be getting a lot of extra treats at one time. If your dog is on a special diet, consult your veterinarian and find out what food treats you can use.

The beauty of clicker training is that it teaches dogs to think. It is a kind, nonviolent way to teach a dog what is expected of her. It is also long-lasting and easy, making it fun for the trainer and trainee alike.

CHAPTER 3

Yes, Drill Sergeant: A Word About Punishment

As humans and as our dog's drill sergeant, we are absolutely convinced that in order to change behavior we must provide some sort of punishment that will eliminate bad behavior altogether: pushups, cleaning the mess hall, etc. In truth, no animals, including humans, respond well to punishment. Although it has been part of training dogs for decades, punishment is not a good or effective way to train a well-behaved family pet.

Punishment Can Make Things Worse

Over time, trainers have found that it is totally unnecessary to use punishment in order to get reliable, acceptable behavior. In many cases, using punishment can actually make some problems worse. Consider these two points:

- Punishment stops behavior, but it does not teach or provide another choice.
- The many negative side effects of punishment outweigh the short-term benefits.

The best human example of why punishment is ineffective is a speeding ticket. If you've ever been pulled over for speeding, you'll understand. The moment the lights flash behind you is horrible. When you're actually pulled over, your heart races, you stutter and stammer, and you wait and wait and wait. Now you've got a fine to pay, and points on your insurance as well. Do you stop speeding? Well, for a little while you do, but one day you are late, you speed again, and you get away with it.

You may have been a little more careful this time, avoiding speed traps and keeping your eyes open, but you were speeding. After being punished severely only weeks before, how could you go back to that behavior? Quite simply, the punishment made you a better speeder! You are no longer a random, careless speeder; you actually look for cruisers and avoid known speed traps. The punishment actually improved the way you speed.

Punishment Is Reactive

The first problem with punishment is that it is a response to bad behavior, whereas training initiates good behavior. The second problem with punishment as a training tool is that you can't always control what the student learns. In fact, punishment puts the subject in an excitable and defensive emotional state, which interferes with the dog's ability to learn anything.

Another reason that punishment is not very effective for fixing behavior problems is that it is only part of the equation. Punishment only stops the unwanted behavior; it does not show the dog what he should have done instead. Punishment occurs too late to teach anything because by the time it is delivered, the dog has already done the undesirable behavior and cannot undo it.

⭐ ABOUT FACE

Your first reaction when your dog does something he should not is not to get angry, yell, and punish. If you come home and your pup has had an accident on the floor and you yell, this does not show your dog that having an accident is bad. It says that when Mommy or Daddy comes home, they are going to get yelled at! Try and control your emotions and understand your puppy.

Punishing your dog for jumping on the company will not make him want to sit in front of them next time. In fact, punishment delivered by a visitor or in the presence of one might actually teach your dog to be fearful of visitors because it's sometimes unpleasant to be around them. This is not what you want to teach. After working so hard to make sure that your dog is social with people, it would be detrimental to all to start punishing him for being friendly.

Timing Is Everything

If you are going to use punishment and have it mean anything, the timing of the correction has to be precise; it must happen the moment the undesirable behavior begins. Not many people, especially the average pet owner, are capable of doing this. Another issue with timing the correction is that the dog is probably overstimulated and excited, which means her brain is not in learning mode. In order to process information, a dog has to be in a fairly relaxed state.

If the timing of the correction were perfect, the dog would need to be rewarded as soon as the inappropriate behavior stopped. The timing of the reward here is the instructive part for the dog. If the behavior that we are trying to fix is one the dog has been practicing for a long time, a very high rate of reinforcement for the right behavior must be employed or the new desirable behavior will not replace the old behavior. Remember that old habits die hard, and it is difficult to adopt new ways of doing things without a being heavily reinforced for the right choices.

Redirect the Behavior

Rather than using corrections (a polite word for "punishment), either redirect or interrupt the dog before he starts the behavior. At the first sign of alert or tension, the dog must be interrupted and redirected to the more appropriate behavior. An interruption could be something like saying the dog's name, or touching the dog on the shoulder, or turning away from whatever captured the dog's interest.

To work effectively, interruptions must be delivered before the dog starts the behavior. In the case of barking, for instance, if you wait until the dog is barking and frantic you will not be able to distract him from what he's barking at in order to teach him anything. For some one-track-minded dogs, you could use a strong correction and it still wouldn't phase him or stop his behavior. It would be like trying to reason with someone who is angry—a person not in a rational frame of mind is not capable of listening to you or being reasonable.

Instead, start paying attention to what triggers the barking, and interrupt the dog while he's still thinking about it. To short-circuit an undesirable behavior, you might have the dog go to his bed, or move further away from the distractions so he's not as excited. Your goal is to interrupt him close to the distractions in the environments where he practices the undesirable behavior, but it is unreasonable to try to train him there in the beginning. As with any constructive and lasting training, you need to start with small, simple steps that enable the dog to be successful.

Establishing New Patterns

In order to stop unwanted behavior and get your dog to develop a new pattern of behavior, you must have not only a set plan to accomplish your goal, but you must also prevent the dog from practicing the old behavior while you are retraining her. Setting up a new pattern of behavior isn't easy for dogs, because they get into habits like we do and tend to do things the same way again and again if we let them.

Repetition

The important thing to remember when changing a pattern is that you need to practice the new pattern over and over and reward the dog repeatedly for the new behavior until she adopts it as her own. In the meantime, if you want to get where you are going faster, you need to stop allowing the dog to reinforce herself for the wrong behavior by preventing it from happening. Stepping on the leash to prevent jumping will not, by itself, teach your dog to sit, but it will reduce her options and make sitting more likely, because that is the only behavior getting rewarded.

An Ounce of Prevention

The more time you spend with dogs, the more you will find that a large part of training is really management. Gates, crates, and pens can be your best friends when raising and training a dog. Although they don't teach the dog not to chew the couch or pee on the carpet, they prevent inappropriate behaviors from becoming bad habits. Managing a dog's environment helps him to be right by limiting his choices. It isn't the solution to all of your behavior problems but it is an integral part of it.

For example, a fence is a management tool for dogs that enjoy playing in their yards and owners who want to keep them there. A baby gate in the kitchen limits the dog's freedom so that he can't get into trouble in the rest of the house. When you don't have time to teach your dog to sit for a guest, putting your dog behind a gate would be a better way to manage his jumping problem than letting him dive on the person or run out the front door.

The Fallout of Punishment: Aggression

If punishment is mistimed or too severe, it can cause the dog to turn and bite whoever is closest. Dogs that are corrected for barking and lunging at other dogs and people don't learn to like them; in fact, many of these animals become unpredictable and dangerous. They learn that the presence of other dogs or people means they are about to get punished, so they will often bite without warning.

Warnings Work for a Reason

If you physically punish a dog for growling he may stop growling and skip right to the bite instead. You have made that dog far more dangerous because he no longer warns people that he is not comfortable, he just bites them. You have, in essence, created a better biter. Growling is a dog's way of warning us that he is uncomfortable and that if the person or dog doesn't go away there's going to be trouble. Punishing the warning doesn't make sense; we want to change the way the dog feels about the person or dog, not take away the warning that he is about to bite. This is nature's way of letting us know we have a problem and gives us time to do something about it (like teach the dog a positive association with people and dogs) before the dog bites.

Training Versus Punishment

Never use punishment with any problem related to aggression around people or dogs—the risk of creating a better biter is just too high. Here are five reasons to teach your dog instead of punish him.

1. Punishment must be repeated frequently to remind the dog to avoid her mistake.
2. Punishment doesn't teach the dog anything; dogs with little confidence will wilt.
3. With punishment, you can't control what the dog learns.
4. Punishment can damage the relationship between owner and dog.

5. Punishment can accelerate aggression by suppressing all precursors to aggression so that the dog skips right to the bite.

There are many reasons for not using punishment in training your dog to be a better companion. In general, punishment misses the point. It comes too late to be instructive and has the danger of teaching the dog to be better at the very behavior we are trying to eliminate.

✪ ABOUT FACE!

If your dog is behaving so poorly that you think she needs punishment, then the real problem is that she needs more information about what she has to do to be right. Instead of spending your time figuring out how to stop the behaviors you don't like, map out what you want the dog to do and retrain her.

If a dog's basic needs for exercise, training, and attention are met and she is carefully managed according to her age and training level, you will have fewer behavioral problems and less to correct. Think carefully about how you use punishment, because it is often an indicator of a much larger issue. If you want a well-behaved dog that responds to you quickly and is fun to be around, don't use punishment to teach her; it won't get you where you want to go.

Give Your Dog a Job

When dealing with behavior problems, it is essential that you plan out what your dog should do in place of the behavior you are trying to eliminate. If you want to change inappropriate behavior permanently, you must replace it with the right behavior and heavily reinforce it or no real change will occur.

Have a Plan

Many dog owners know exactly what they don't want their dogs to do but very few have given much thought to what the dog should do instead. Leaving your dog with too many choices may lead to your dog choosing incorrectly and you being frustrated that he's not "getting it," which is unfair to both of you.

In order to have a dog that is trained to be responsive and enjoyable, you will need to get your family's act together. The fastest way to change your dog's unwanted behavior is to stop reinforcing the incorrect behavior and start reinforcing an alternative behavior in its place. There are endless possibilities to choose from. Try to come up with ideas about how you want your dog to respond in different situations.

When choosing which behaviors to reinforce, you'll want to keep these certain points in mind:

- Keep it simple.
- Choose something incompatible with the wrong behavior.
- Plan and be prepared (carry your treats and clicker with you).
- Control variables (such as distractions and the environment).
- Avoid reinforcing the wrong behavior.
- Build a bank account for good behavior.
- Teach your dog to perform this behavior anywhere.

Every time the dog gets to practice the old, undesirable behavior he is putting money in the bank for doing that behavior again. Preventing the wrong behavior from happening is half of the training.

Keep It Simple

Whatever you choose as the alternate behavior should be simple for the dog to offer quickly and reliably. Choose a single behavior, like Sit or Down, and reinforce it often. If the behavior is too complicated or involved, your dog may lose interest and go back to the undesirable behavior. A simple behavior like Sit is something you are likely to notice and reinforce even in a distracting environment.

Choose an Incompatible Behavior

Make sure that the new behavior is incompatible with the undesirable behavior. For instance, a dog cannot sit and jump at the same time. If you reinforce sitting as the desirable behavior when your dog greets new people, it won't be long before your dog doesn't even try to jump. Be forewarned: Replacing jumping with sitting takes lots of time and practice before the dog will offer it on her own. Practice in short, frequent sessions and as opportunities present themselves from day to day. Remember, preventing jumping as an option by putting your foot on the leash will help your dog to be right more often.

Plan Ahead for Success

If you want a well-trained dog that responds to your commands everywhere, you have to train it everywhere. Dogs pick things up quickly, but are lousy generalizers, tending to revert back to old, ingrained behaviors in new environments. If you haven't taught your dog to sit when greeting strangers at the park, he will not try that as his first choice of behaviors. Always be ready to reinforce the right behavior and prevent the wrong one from happening as best you can. Have a leash hanging by the door so that you are ready to prevent jumping on guests, and have a container of treats ready to reinforce sitting.

If you're not prepared to train, don't allow your dog to greet the visitor. If you want to fix behavior that is deeply rooted, you have to combat it with well-timed repetitions, a high rate of rewards, and frequent practice around distractions. It may seem awkward at first to carry your clicker and treats with you all the time, but it is essential to capture the moment your dog makes the right choice.

Overall, learning this way is more like real life for the dog, and the learning tends to become more permanent because the dog begins to realize that her commands work everywhere. The more distractions she gets to practice around, the quicker she will learn to generalize her response to your commands.

Control the Variables

Controlling the variables means controlling what's shifting your dog's attention away from you. Distractions often ruin the best-laid plans simply because they are too stimulating for the dog to ignore. If you control the frequency, type, and distance of the distractions, you will increase the speed with which your dog learns. If ringing the doorbell sends your dog into a frenzy, you may want to work on desensitizing him to the doorbell sound first; then you can move on to actually greeting the visitor. In this example, the dog's response to the doorbell and the dog's response to the person would be considered two separate issues.

Other variables might include things that move, like balls, off-leash dogs, cars, kids, runners, or environmental factors like being outside, or the presence of food. The key points to keep in mind for getting your dog to be successful around these distractions is controlling the distance between your dog and the distraction, and controlling the intensity of the distraction. In order for your dog's training program to be successful, you need to find your dog's critical distance, and work from there.

⭐ ABOUT FACE!

The distance at which he notices the distraction but will still perform the behavior is the starting point. Then, in subsequent training sessions, decrease that distance until he is able to work while the distractions are close by. You will immediately notice that the distance between your dog and the action is an important factor in the success of your training sessions. If the dog is overstimulated by the distraction, he will not be able to ignore it and will not perform the behaviors you ask of him.

The second point to keep in mind when working around distractions is to pay attention to how much of a distraction you are working with. To decrease the intensity of a distraction, offer less movement, fewer dogs, people, kids, or other visual stimuli before attempting to teach the dog anything. As your dog starts to learn to ignore distractions and perform the behavior well, you can gradually increase the intensity until he is working in the middle of the distraction.

As you train your dog to respond to you regardless of where you are and what is happening, your goal over time is to decrease the distance and increase the intensity of the distractions so that your dog will pay attention to you and respond to you regardless of what else is going on. Doing this in a slow sequence of progressions will help you attain your goals more quickly and reliably.

Prevention Is Half the Cure

Human nature is to notice what is going wrong and point it out. When trying to change behavior in animals, putting pressure upon an animal to change the choices it has made is a waste of time since the animal cannot change the past anymore than you can.

If you want to make a difference in a future behavior, you must set up the animal for success. Set up an animal for success by limiting her options, providing good consequences for the correct choices, and preventing or providing negative consequences for the wrong choices. Because the animal has choices, the learning is more permanent and the consequences will directly shape her response.

Pointing out a mistake acts as reinforcement and can actually teach the person or animal to make that same mistake over and over again. A much better approach to changing behavior permanently is to avoid reinforcing the wrong behavior in the first place and, if possible, preventing it from actually happening. It is important during the teaching phase to avoid giving the dog any attention for the wrong behavior, and concentrate on noticing what's going right. This also means that you should be ready to reward the unexpected good behavior your dog offers anytime it happens. If you're not prepared to click and treat, then shower your pup with lots of praise and pats, or games and opportunities.

Generalization . . . Taking It on the Road

Taking it on the road means getting your dog to respond to all of his commands in new environments by training your dog everywhere. Generalization refers to the dog being able to perform the behavior regardless of the distractions. Dogs need your help to get them on track in new environments.

The best way to help a dog whose behavior falls apart in a new environment is to go back to kindergarten. Help the dog perform the behavior with a treat or toy as a lure. The idea is to drill the dog for five to ten repetitions to get him working again and then wean him off of the extra help. Repeating the command when the dog is obviously too distracted to hear what you are saying is not teaching the dog anything but how to ignore you. With a little patience and practice, it won't be long before your dog understands that his training works everywhere, regardless of the distraction.

Solutions to Breed-Specific Behavior Problems

Dogs with persistent behavior problems are often exhibiting behavior that is related to the job they were bred to do. When a dog has a behavior problem related to its original working ability, think of it as hard-wired behavior, or behavior that a dog's genetics have preprogrammed him to do. Consider the Border collie that chases and nips at heels, the retriever obsessed with having everything in her mouth, or the terrier that barks or chases squirrels. In these cases the genetics of the dog determine her behavior, because it is a behavior that the dog was bred to do, such as herding, retrieving, guarding, or chasing things that move.

Constant and Patient Reinforcement

What hard-wiring means for you is that without the appropriate training and practice, it will be harder to stop the dog from practicing the undesirable behavior. There are several things to keep in mind when you are retraining dogs like this:

- Keep the rate of reinforcement high.
- Build up your dog's bank account for good behavior.
- Train your dog to perform the behavior for a longer period of time.
- Consider teaching a trick as a replacement behavior.

If you are going to change the dog's mind about a behavior that is this instinctive, you need to provide lots of reinforcement for the behavior you are trying to teach instead. A high rate of reinforcement means that you keep your standards low and reward the dog for even attempting the new behavior. You don't up your criteria or expect multiple repetitions; you simply reward the new behavior as often as possible. This way it will be more likely for your dog to respond to a given situation with the right behavior because it has been rewarded so frequently.

⭐ ABOUT FACE!

It is extremely important that you exercise patience with your recruited puppy when he behaves in the way his hardwiring dictates. You cannot punish a dog for doing what it has been programmed to do—but you can try and alter the behavior through patience and training.

Each reward for the new behavior is money in the bank. You are building a reinforcement history that has to compete with a natural and self-rewarding behavior. Building a strong reinforcement history takes time and practice before it will eventually replace the old hard-wired behavior with the new desirable one.

Practice Makes Perfect

The more you work with your dog, the fewer behavior problems you will have. You are spending time building up a history of "training equals fun!" Teaching your dog to perform is a great way to help you get to know your dog and improve your relationship with him; plus, training tricks is fun and most people enjoy spending time training their dogs this way.

Some dogs love learning tricks more than anything else, so they are more willing to work longer and perform with enthusiasm. If you prefer to teach your dog tricks, why not use them in everyday life to help prevent your dog from practicing inappropriate behaviors? If your dog is a puller, how about mixing in Roll Overs, Sit Up, or Spin with reinforcing the dog for staying with you. In order to use tricks to replace problem behavior, not only does the dog have to know the trick very well in all different kinds of environments, she also has to be heavily reinforced (at least initially) for choosing to perform the trick rather than the inappropriate behavior. The more you practice what you want, the better it will happen for you when you truly need it. The more creative you are in your training program, the better your relationship with your dog will be.

CHAPTER 4

Minor Infractions: When Your Recruit Is Just Being a Puppy

So, you thought your puppy's boot camp would be full of Kodak moments—and instead the alert was elevated because you've got a miniature terrorist on your hands. Does it seem like all your puppy does is get into or cause trouble? Is he playing too rough with your kids, barking or crying too often, roughly jumping onto people and making a speedway out of your home?

A Puppy Is a Puppy Is a Puppy

The first thing to remember is that a recruited puppy is first and foremost a puppy, and not a soldier. Does that mean you just have to grin and bear this trying time? Of course not. But it does mean you need to look at and understand your puppy for what he is: a baby learning about the world. Like human babies, puppies explore with their mouths, their paws (hands), and all their senses. They are soaking up everything about their environment, including how their littermates and the "adults" in their world respond to it. If something's exciting to others in their pack, it'll be exciting to your puppy; if something smells good, tastes good, or feels good, he wants a part of it.

So what are you going to do about it? Like any good parent, your job is to teach your puppy the rules. Not by yelling, hitting, choking, or hurting your puppy—which only makes him afraid of you—but by truly teaching. Knowing what you want your puppy to do is the first step. Then set up small but achievable goals that you and your puppy can celebrate together.

Problem-Solving Mindset

To teach your puppy good manners, which should minimize problems, remember the following: Teach fairly and wisely. Be the role model for your puppy (and your family).

Ask yourself how you're contributing to the problem. Remember, it's only a problem if you think it's a problem; your puppy doesn't think digging in the yard is a problem, he thinks it's fun.

Common Puppy Problems

These are the problems you're most likely to experience as a new puppy owner.

Mouthing and Nipping

Even if you've only had your puppy one day, you've learned that he explores things with his mouth. This is completely natural; he can't help it! If your puppy came from a sizeable litter, he learned to roughhouse and play with his littermates using his mouth, body, and paws. So his mouth is his direct access to everything pleasurable, and his method of saying, "Enough" or "Back off." What you have to discourage is your puppy using his mouth to "maul" you or anyone with the sharpness of his teeth or the strength of his jaws. Here's how.

If your puppy chomps down too hard on your finger, hand, wrist, ankle—any body part—immediately cry out in pain. Say, "OUCH," and make it sound like you just got your entire limb bitten off by a shark. Don't raise your voice in anger. Don't strike out at your puppy. Don't shake your limb or pull it away from your puppy's mouth. Just let out a big YELP. That should surprise him enough so that he stops pressing down and looks up at you.

As soon as your puppy releases you, change your tone completely and warmly (not excitedly) praise your puppy. Hopefully you have a toy available nearby. Give that to him and tell him what a good puppy he is to take the toy. Instructed this way, most puppies quickly learn bite inhibition.

The biggest problem with a mouthy puppy and a family is that while it might be easy for you to control yourself and respond correctly when puppy gets you with those razor-sharp puppy teeth, it's usually not the way children respond. Their natural tendency is to pull away from the puppy or flail at the puppy—both behaviors that may incite the puppy to increase his attempts to nip because he thinks this is rough play.

Teach your children how to react to this situation by staging it with your puppy and demonstrating to them the response you want them to exhibit. Your puppy and your children will learn at the same time.

⊛ ABOUT FACE!

Children are a lot like puppies in the way they need to be taught. Just like a child won't understand anything but the puppy's bite and how she wants to get away from it, a puppy won't understand anything but how he wants to play and suddenly everyone is yelling. Both puppy and child walk away from this situation with the same thought: playing together is bad. This is not something you want to teach!

Crying and Whining

Believe it or not, in the barracks, this behavior can be more annoying than nipping and housetraining. Why? Because it's so hard for your puppy to understand what you want him to stop doing when he's crying or whining. The best remedy is to completely ignore your complaining pup when he's doing either of these things.

It will be very difficult for you. After all, a crying recruit is like a crying baby—your instinct tells you to go and do what you can to relieve whatever the discomfort is that's causing the crying or whining. Remember the old adage that dogs do things to get what they want. If your dog has been adequately fed, exercised, and loved, the only other thing he could want is more attention, more food, or more exercise. But he's not the one who should be dictating that, because next thing you know he may decide he wants to stroll the block at 3 A.M. No, your puppy gets the things he needs because you oversee his environment responsibly enough so that his needs are taken care of. Therefore, crying and whining become behaviors whose sole purpose is to get your attention.

However, the second he stops crying (eventually he has to stop), go to him and reward him with attention, exercise, or food. If you're trying to break a habitual cry or whine, you'll need to increase the time between when your dog stops and when you go to him so that he truly associates that he's being praised for being quiet. Another solution to crying or whining is to startle the puppy. This doesn't have to be a physical force correction; instead, it's intended solely to break the offensive action and try to redirect the behavior.

ABOUT FACE!

Don't become a slave to your puppy! If your puppy is crying or whining for no apparent reason other than to get you to pay attention to him, try turning on a radio or television to block out the sound of his protestations. As hard as it will be, ignore your puppy's cries.

Chewing

The mess hall. The obstacle course. The table. The chairs. The rug. The sofa. The car seats. The kids' toys. The garden hose. The swimming pool cover. The remote control. A cell phone. You name it and a dog has chewed it to bits. Is there a worse feeling than coming home and seeing your beloved sound asleep amid a cyclone of destruction? After all, you feed him, exercise him, buy him great toys, comfy beds, keep him up on his shots, and love him to pieces. And this is what you get in return?

You're not going to want to hear this, but 99 percent of the time the destruction is your fault. You allowed the puppy too much freedom while alone in the house. You didn't provide any puppy-friendly chew toys. You left the puppy alone too long. You left one of your favorite "things" (cell phone, remote, handbag, shoes, pillow, etc.) within reach of your inquisitive puppy—and don't underestimate the reach of a bored puppy.

What do you do when this happens? Yell at your puppy? Spank or shove your puppy? Isolate your puppy (to "show him")? No, no, no. Please—for your sake and your puppy's. The first thing to do is take your puppy outside. He will probably need to relieve himself after all the fun he's had and the stuff he's eaten. If possible, leave him outside in a fenced area while you go back in to survey the damage. Make sure immediately that your puppy hasn't eaten anything that could be poisonous (prescription drugs, household cleaners, some houseplants) or damaging to sensitive body organs (pins, splintered bones, large buttons). If you find any remnants of anything dangerous in the debris, call your veterinarian immediately and ask him or her if you need to bring your puppy in for an examination.

If the damage is just, well, damage, bring your puppy inside and put him in his crate. While you're cleaning up, you will probably want to cry or curse. That's okay, just don't direct it at your puppy. He'll pick up how upset you are, and if he thinks he's the cause, he may worry that you will always react this way to him. Then you have a puppy who hasn't learned anything except that Mommy or Daddy is scary when they come home, which will make the puppy more anxious, which will lead to more destructive chewing.

After you've cleaned up, assess how your puppy was able to get to what he got into. Did you leave the garbage can where he could tip it over? Did you think it was safe to confine him to the kitchen and the den now that he's older? Lesson learned: don't do it again.

What you want to do is make sure that your puppy has chew toys he's really interested in. Smear peanut butter in a rubber Kong. That'll keep him busy. Add different sizes of treats and kibble so they fall out gradually over the course of a few hours or the day. (Remember to subtract this amount of food from his regular meals.) Get a cube or round toy that you can put treats into and that puppy needs to bat around to get the treats out. Puppies are most prone to get into trouble just after we leave and just before we come home. They miss us when we go and get excited to see us later. This time can seem like an eternity. But you can have your puppy loving to see you leave and well-behaved when you come home by getting him hooked on safe chews that earn tasty rewards.

Playing Too Rough

Many owners say their dog's favorite game is tug-of-war. And for many owners it's pretty fun, too—until your once-fifteen-pound fluff ball is seventy pounds of adolescent muscle and will do any-thing to win. Or until he starts to growl whenever you come near any of his toys. This doesn't mean you can't play tug-of-war. It just means that, like everything else, you have to call the shots. You determine when the game begins and when it ends. This is where "Drop it" comes in handy again. If tug-of-war is turning into war, say "Drop it" and stop pulling. If he doesn't let go right away, don't pull again. Say "Drop it" again. If he doesn't, get up and walk away. It's you he wants to play with. Don't turn his resilience into a contest of wills. When he has dropped it, without saying anything, go get the tug toy and put it away where he can't reach or find it by himself.

If you keep tug games short and in control from the very beginning, you and your dog will be able to enjoy them within appropriate limits. Make sure the rest of your family understands these tug game rules, too.

ABOUT FACE!

As with rough play, make sure your entire family is familiar with and participates actively in your pup's training regiment. If Mommy or Daddy does not stop bad behavior, then who do you think the puppy is going to want to be with more? Yes, the one that lets her tear up the house and pee on the floor. It can also lead to confusion for your dog and the training will be for naught!

The same goes for any kind of rough-housing, whether you're doing it with a toy, your hands, rolling on the floor, whatever. Start with fun, short sessions, and when you've had enough, say, "That's all," and calmly stop whatever you're doing.

Playing with Other Puppies

Rough play among puppies is usually harmless amusement for humans and canines. If generally friendly and tolerant of one another, puppies rarely inflict injury. They will get noisy and animated: growling, barking, squealing, tumbling, and dragging one another by convenient body parts (like ears and limbs) is common. Break them up only if one is being endangered or if the play occurs in a formal living room or while people desire quiet. Don't raise your voice to break them up. Instead, leash one or both puppies and give a subdued command to stop, then enticingly lure your puppy away from the action and reward him for following you by giving him a treat and telling him what a good boy he is.

Separation Anxiety

Having to leave a dog alone is worrisome if he gets frantically frustrated when he's separated from his owner. Overly dependent dogs commonly respond to separations by continually barking, whining, and howling, destroying his living space, and attempting to escape by chewing, digging, and jumping over fences and out of windows. In addition to causing expensive damage, many dogs injure themselves. When panicked, they are oblivious to the physical discomforts of laryngitis, bloody-raw gums and paws, broken teeth, self-mutilation caused by chewing and licking, and even broken limbs as a result of jumping out of windows.

How are you supposed to live with a puppy that holds you hostage by not being able to be left alone? Here's my advice: Avoid both after-the-fact corrections, which increase anxiety, and consoling tones or gentle petting, which reinforce the neurosis. Instead:

- Exercise your puppy vigorously and regularly.
- Improve his ability to handle all sources of stress by teaching reliable obedience.
- As you come and go, remain relaxed and refrain from addressing your dog.

- To directly increase his tolerance of separations, practice these three exercises:

   1. **Random tie-outs:** Insist that he remain quiet when you leave. Take your dog to indoor and outdoor areas, familiar and unfamiliar, filled with or absent of distractions. Silently tie his leash short to a stationary object and walk away for a few minutes. Sometimes remain in sight and other times walk out of sight. When you do return to him, praise him for being a good puppy. Practice every other day for a half hour until he'll be silent regardless of where you leave him, where you go, and how long you're gone.

   2. **Out-of-sight sit- and down-stays.** This is the same principle as the previous exercise, except you're asking your puppy to stay sitting or lying down as you leave for increasing amounts of time. Don't expect a puppy younger than six months old to be able to sit and stay for longer than a minute or so, same with staying down. But as you work with your puppy on the out-of-sight exercise, you can get in an occasional sit-stay or down-stay, and reward him for doing so. As your puppy gets older, you can increase the lengths of time you ask your puppy to stay seated or down.

   3. **Whirling dervish departures:** Dash from room to room grabbing your keys, briefcase, jacket, lunch box, etc. Rush out the door and to your car then back out of the driveway, motor around the block, pull back in the garage, and

saunter into the house. As you put your things away, completely ignore your puppy. After relaxing for a few minutes, repeat the frenzied departure and relaxed arrival over and over for an hour. Repeat this pattern three times the first week, then once a week for a month.

To reinforce your training, make it a habit to periodically confine your puppy while you're at home. Sequester him in a quiet area and place your recently worn sweatshirt or bathrobe on the floor on the other side of the closed door. If your smell permeates his room, he may not even realize it when you finally do leave. Give him his favorite toy only when you confine him. Then, when you do actually leave, follow the same routine.

Begging, Stealing, and Scavenging

It often takes only one tidbit for your clever puppy to be convinced that your meals are better than his and that you're willing to share if he begs. If you've fostered this bad habit, it can be broken, but you probably can't be cured. You have to stop feeding him ANY human food any time around mealtime. I know your puppy is your best buddy, and if you've enjoyed your pizza, why not give him some of the crust? It sure makes him happy! The answer is: be aware of the repercussions. Don't expect your puppy to differentiate from the times you eat a pizza in front of the tube and gladly share it with him and the time you have your daughter's soccer team over for pizza and you don't want him underfoot or being fed by every member of the team and then getting sick.

Differentiate your mealtimes and his by confining him in his crate or a separate room where he can't watch you while you eat. Give him a favorite toy so he's distracted and doesn't whine, cry, drool, or stare you down. Stay strong!

If you were all alone in someone else's house, what would you do when you got bored? Would the thought of looking at their stuff or even rummaging through cabinets, closets, or the refrigerator tempt you?

Now you know how a dog feels. He is trapped and bored and has no hands with which to do arts and crafts, but he does have plenty of senses yearning to be indulged. When given too much freedom too soon, he will discover the joys of hunting for household treasures too often left easily accessible by negligent humans.

Many dogs steal for amusement when you're home. They know the only guaranteed way to rouse you from the recliner is to show off the valuables that have been confiscated. Police your canine kleptomaniac by:

- Incarceration—crating
- Chain gang—umbilical-cording (keeping your pup on a leash, even in the house!)
- Surveillance—keeping your eyes glued to him

Don't be a victim, keep the garbage out of reach, close cabinets and closets, and put laundry away, teach the "Drop it" or "Leave it" command, and dispense justice fairly. Only correct crimes in progress, never correct stealing after the fact. Upon discovering the infraction, leash your dog, invite him to make the same mistake, and correct it by redirecting his attention to something he needs to do to get a reward, such as praise and/or treats from mom.

Problem Prevention

Giving an untrained puppy freedom in your house can be deadly. Natural curiosity and boredom cause them to chew electrical cords, ingest toxic substances, and destroy valuables. When given freedom too soon, puppies who don't accidentally execute themselves often become homeless because of damage the owner is angry about but could have and should have prevented. Puppies are opportunists. This doesn't mean they are bad; it just means we are foolish if we walk out of the room leaving goodies on the table and believe our puppies would never think about touching them.

If you don't know where your puppy is, he is probably into something he shouldn't be. Save your valuables, your sanity, and your puppy by watching his every move, umbilical cording him, or confining him to a safe, destruction-proof area.

⭐ ABOUT FACE!

Don't think your puppy will want to chew less if he's by himself outside or in his crate. He'll get bored just as quickly in these spots as he will be in the living room if he doesn't have something to chew on to take his mind off things.

So, in the course of your puppy's boot camp, please keep these simple puppy issues in mind. Your recruit isn't defying you, he's just being the puppy that he is.

CHAPTER 5

Drop and Give Me Twenty, Pup: Barking and Jumping Problems

Just as you open your mouth to shout some orders at your recruit, dogs bark to communicate with us and with each other. However, excessive barking is inappropriate and a symptom of a larger problem. If a dog barks excessively it means that the dog's mental, emotional, and physical needs are not being met. This problem must be addressed first, before peace and quiet reign.

Why Do Dogs Bark Excessively?

A barking dog is a common problem among dog owners and is often the top complaint of neighbors who listen to the restless protests of a dog confined to a yard and bored to death. Dogs are pack animals with strong bonds to their family members; it is unnatural for them to be alone for hours at a time. In their boredom and frustration they tend to bark, which is self-reinforcing. Barking is an emotional release, a way for a dog to express its emotion and let out bottled-up anxiety and frustration. Excessive barking is a symptom of a larger issue. In general it means that the dog needs something that she isn't getting or is being consistently reinforced for the wrong behavior.

 ABOUT FACE!

A dog that barks too much falls into one of three categories: the dog that barks when left alone; the dog that barks at visitors, noise, and people passing by while you are home; and lastly the dog that barks at you for attention.

Meet Your Dog's Needs

All dogs need a healthy diet, a predictable schedule, lots of exercise, interaction with people and other dogs, training, a safe place to sleep and rest, and a stimulating environment with toys and things to chew. Dogs also need to be taught from the time they are puppies to be content when they are away from you.

Dogs that are with their owners all the time (perhaps you work from home or are a stay-at-home parent) can also become excessive barkers when their owners do leave them even briefly. These dogs become inappropriately bonded to their owners and in their absence find it difficult to cope with being alone. This overattachment between owner and dog can erode the dog's self-confidence and contentment when they are alone. Take a moment to examine how much or how little time you spend with your dog and make the necessary adjustments to help her feel confident and secure.

Mindful Management

The next few sections review some basic elements of what you need to keep in mind while you come up with a plan to curb (or at least cut down) your dog's barking. The philosophy is the same for training any behavior: have a plan, be patient, be consistent, and reinforce the right behaviors.

Doin' What Comes Naturally

Some breeds are prone to barking, but all dogs can learn not to bark excessively or inappropriately. If you have a dog that is known for barking, nip the problem in the bud while the dog is still a pup. Some dogs were bred for their ability to chase or guard, and barking is sometimes part of the package.

If you know what sets your dog off into a frenzy of barking, think carefully about how you can prevent these episodes from happening. The more barking your dog does, the more she gets reinforced for barking. The more reinforcement a behavior gets, the more likely the behavior is to occur and become stronger. If you want to have a quieter household, you need to find your dog's triggers for barking and short circuit as many of them as you can.

Set a Reasonable Goal

A dog that barks a lot isn't going to just quit one day when you find the magic cure. Barking is reinforcing to dogs and often gets worse before it gets better. Sit down with your family and set a reasonable goal for your dog. Maybe your dog is the type that barks when the doorbell rings; in this case, your goal might be that she's allowed to bark for thirty seconds and then she must be quiet when you tell her to be quiet. Or if she hears a noise, she can let you know something's going on but then must stop barking and go to her bed. It really doesn't matter what the goal is, so long as it is simple and fairly easy for the dog to do.

It is your job to sit down, agree on something reasonable, and teach it to the dog. Don't be afraid to set small goals and build up the time the dog is required to be quiet by seconds. It isn't reasonable to expect a dog that has been barking excessively for years to suddenly quit overnight.

Find the Antecedents to Barking

An antecedent is the trigger or the cause of a behavior. For instance, your dog barks at the sound of a knock at the door or the doorbell. The knock or doorbell would be considered the antecedent for the behavior of barking. Knowing what triggers your dog's barking can be crucial to teaching her to be quiet. The pattern or chain of reaction goes like this: antecedent, behavior, consequence, appropriate behavior, reward. You need to complete this entire circuit of behavior in order to teach your dog not to bark excessively.

A good way to find antecedents is to keep a chart of when your dog barks and what happens right before she barks. Write down exactly what you think triggered the barking and time how long it took her to stop. If you time how long it takes your dog to calm down, you will know when you are making progress in your training program and when you are spinning your wheels. You'll know you're on track if the number of seconds it takes your dog to calm down becomes smaller over time. Good drill sergeants chart progress to see results!

Set the Consequences

For dogs that keep at it and barely take a breath between barks, you may want to use something to interrupt them. You will be stopping the barking for a second so that you can reward him for being quiet. A consequence is the same as punishment, so alone it will only stop the behavior—it will not teach the dog what it should do instead.

Some ideas for consequences might be a squirt of water, a loud noise, shaking a can of pennies, a nonelectric no-bark collar (this device is worn around the neck and distracts the dog by squirting a blast of citronella when she barks). Consequences would be used to interrupt the behavior of excessive barking to get the dog to stop for a second so that it could be rewarded for being quiet. You will want to plan out ahead of time what the dog should do instead of bark so that you know what behavior to reinforce.

Notice the Right Stuff

Too often with a noisy dog, we tend to only notice when they are barking and not when they are quiet. A good part of the solution for barking is catching and reinforcing the dog for being quiet. Each reinforcement you provide for a quiet behavior will be money in the bank for a quieter dog overall. Pay attention to your dog at times like this by petting or playing with him, giving a treat, bringing him inside, letting him outside, opening the crate door, and so on. Whatever would be reinforcing at the moment, reward your dog with it and you will notice that your dog barks less over the course of several days or weeks (depending on the value of the reinforcement and the severity of the problem).

Get Set for Success

If you live in a busy neighborhood, be smart—letting your dog have unsupervised free access to your yard is not a good idea. He will only find things to bark at, reinforcing his obnoxious behavior over and over. This poor management is money in the bank for more barking, because dogs think that barking is fun and will continue in the absence of anything better to occupy their time. Setting up your dog to succeed means that you use prevention to help your dog to be quiet, and then make sure you notice and reward him for *being* quiet. Here are some tips for setting your dog up to succeed.

Exercise. A dog can never have too much. Try play dates with other dogs, games of fetch, Frisbee, hide-and-seek, doggie day care, dog walkers, or anyone who will exercise your dog for you.

Keep occupied. Try interesting toys, bones, and chew treats that let your dog exercise his jaws. Dogs that bark are often big chewers, so make sure your dog has plenty of good stuff to chew.

Pay attention. Be there to supervise and redirect your dog. When you are present in the yard, for instance, practice calling your dog away from what he is barking at and reward him for engaging in a different behavior.

Keep him busy. Stuff hollow toys with peanut butter and dry dog food, and hide them all over the house and yard; this will give him something to do while you are out.

Remove the antecedent. Prevent barking as often as possible by blocking his view with shrubs, closing the blinds, or rearranging the furniture. Not allowing your dog to practice the wrong behavior is more than half the cure.

Meet his needs. Have a schedule and stick to it as much as possible. Hire a professional dog walker or a doggie day care to help you with walks and exercise if necessary. The more predictable your dog's routine, the better it is for him. Try to feed, walk, and play with your dog on a predictable schedule so that he will learn to trust you and feel secure.

Be ready. It is very important to be ready to reinforce what's going right. Make a plan with your family and stick to it. The more you know what you want, the more likely you are to get it.

Use a marker signal. The use of a clicker to identify for the dog which behavior is rewardable (the quiet behavior) is crucial information for the dog, and it is difficult to provide it any other way. Remember that the click marks the quiet behavior so you can then follow through with the reward.

Dogs That Bark at Visitors

Dogs that go berserk over visitors may be fearful, overexcited, or downright aggressive to people entering your home. Trying to train the dog to like visitors while also trying to greet your guest is dangerous and will probably be only limitedly successful. A new pattern of behavior is necessary to teach the dog to respond to visitors in a more appropriate way.

If your dog is aggressive or fearful of strangers, you will probably want to enlist the help of a qualified professional dog trainer or behaviorist to help you evaluate your dog and correctly identify the problem. This person will also help you set up training sessions to help your dog learn better greeting manners and be safe doing it. The biggest task to be tackled is to change your dog's mind about how she feels about company.

1. Put the dog out of the room and let your company come in and sit down.
2. After about ten minutes, let your dog out and have everyone ignore her.
3. Arm each person with yummy treats and have visitors drop those treats all around their feet.
4. Let your dog be the one to go to the visitor for the treats.

Congratulations! You just performed your first huge deposit for stopping barking at visitors. Repeat this as often as you can with lots of different people until your dog begins to look forward to having company at the door. You may want to practice this scenario with your own family first, to teach the dog this new pattern of behavior and to help the family members learn a new way of managing the dog around company.

If you're not prepared to train your dog on a given occasion, remove her from the stimuli so at least you're not reinforcing the old pattern of behavior and losing ground. Putting the dog in a separate room or her crate will at least make sure she doesn't fall back to her old ways.

Friendly Options

Dogs that bark because they are happy to see company simply need a distraction to keep them quiet. Teaching your dog to grab a stuffed animal on his way to the door will keep his mouth busy and make it impossible for him to bark and hold the toy at the same time. This is what is meant by teaching your dog to do something that is incompatible with barking.

 **ABOUT FACE**

You can even leave a basket of toys by the door and let your visitor select one to greet your dog with. This will teach your dog that visitors are fun but that barking isn't part of that fun.

Take advantage of any willing helpers like neighbors, fellow dog lovers, and friends. The more your dog gets to practice greeting guests quietly, the better for everyone. Take your time and experiment with different toys to see which ones become your dog's favorites and keep him so engrossed that he forgets to bark!

Taming Doorbell Madness

Dogs that burst into action at the sound of the doorbell will need some help in getting over this huge stimulus before they can be expected to be quiet. The sound of the doorbell ringing may be your dog's antecedent to barking and the most difficult of distractions for her. Most dogs with this problem explode into a cacophony of shrill barking and take several minutes to calm down.

The best way to manage these dogs is to teach them an alternative response to the ringing doorbell. The easiest and noisiest way to do this is through a process called "flooding." Flooding involves ringing the doorbell a billion times when no one is there for the dog to greet so that it eventually doesn't mean what the dog thinks it means. She will start to develop an alternative response to the doorbell and come to expect something different than what she originally thought.

You can also add a bit of classical conditioning to change the dog's association with the doorbell. Classical conditioning is about developing associations between a noise or object, in this case the doorbell, and something good, like a treat or a game of fetch. To incorporate conditioning into the training, ring the bell and shower the dog with treats or start throwing a ball around regardless of the dog's behavior (barking or not).

Here, we are not requiring the dog to do something before she gets something. To the novice trainer, it may seem at first that we are rewarding the dog for barking when we ring the bell and treat the dog. In reality we are trying to form an association between the doorbell and something good so that eventually instead of barking, your dog will be expecting a treat, a game, a toy, or a pat from the visitor. This can be a very powerful tool in trying to change your dog's association with doorbells. Using it to help solve your barking problem may get you where you want to go faster than through other methods.

Dogs That Bark for Attention

Some dogs have their owners all figured out. Remember that most dogs don't work for a living and have nothing else to do but sit around and watch you. They know just what to do to get what they want by barking at you until they get it. When a dog barks at you for attention, it usually means that he is confused about who's in charge in the family and may not have enough rules and limits put upon him to give him a clue as to where he falls in the family hierarchy.

The one thing that almost always works for these needy dogs is to stop paying attention to them when they are barking and to start noticing, marking, and rewarding them for being quiet. Walk away, turn your head to the side, or turn your back on your dog to let him know that what he is doing is not rewardable. If your dog is used to getting his way by barking, this method of management may take a while, but overall it is a faster process and more productive than constantly yelling at the dog to be quiet.

Head Halters

You will find several types of training equipment you can use to shorten your training time that gently help your dog relax and trust that you are in charge. The Gentle Leader Headcollar is one such head halter. Head halters are excellent equipment to own and with the proper introduction, they will cut your training time in half.

The original purpose of the head halter is to teach dogs not to pull, by guiding them under the chin. In essence, when a dog is wearing one of these you control his forward movement by controlling his head. The head halter has an added benefit, too: When fitted correctly, it puts gentle pressure on two points on the dog's head and neck, which help relax the dog and makes him feel more secure.

Some dogs find the effect so calming that they forget to bark and are overall more relaxed and mellow. Head halters should be introduced very slowly if they are to be a useful tool for you. Dogs need to be taught to wear a head halter, but once they like wearing them, it can have an amazing effect on their behavior.

Canine Massage

An often-overlooked method of achieving a quieter dog is canine massage. The massage technique most worthy of mention for changing unwanted behavior is called Tellington Touch, or T-touch. It was started on horses by a woman named Linda Tellington-Jones, and has been applied to all kinds of animals for all kinds of behavior problems.

Dogs hold a lot of their emotions in their face and mouth areas, and most dogs that are tense or hyperactive tend to bark and chew to relieve anxiety. In general, dogs that are restless, overactive, aggressive, or excessive barkers often have a chewing or biting problem as well. These animals can benefit from a bit of therapeutic massage on their muzzles and gum lines.

The best T-touch technique involves making small circles on the muzzle and jaw line with the tips of the fore- and middle fingers. You'll want to lightly move the skin in a clockwise direction for a full circle, then pick your hand up and do another circle right next to it. Take your time and make each circle for a count of five and remember to breathe.

You may want to start getting your dog used to this by sitting on a chair or the floor and having your dog sit between your feet. Support under his jaw with one hand while you make circles with the other. Use a light pressure, about as much as would be comfortable if you made a circle on your eyelid. You can even slip your finger under the dog's lip and make small circles on the gum line itself. You may want to wet your fingers first if your dog has a dry mouth.

There's Always Hope for the Problem Barker

Barking can be problematic for owners and neighbors alike, but it doesn't have to be. Owning a pet should be an enjoyable experience, and barking should not get in the way of you and your family enjoying your pet: the time to act is now. The longer you let your dog reward herself by getting what she wants when she barks, the more barking you will have to listen to.

Put together a training plan that will help reform your barking lunatic into the quiet companion you've always wanted. You have the tools to change the behavior, now it's time to get to work. Take the time to look seriously at the ways in which you are meeting your dog's basic needs for exercise; changing this by increasing your dog's playtime with other dogs is often a huge factor in cutting down on the amount of barking you are listening to. Most of all, don't give up. Even the most obnoxious barker can be taught to be a quieter, more enjoyable companion; he just needs to be trained.

Jumping

A common behavior problem that dog owners have to deal with is their dogs jumping on people. Sometimes the owner of a jumping maniac may stop having visitors because the jumping is so intense. Jumping is natural, for certain breeds, but your dog must function acceptably both in your home and in public.

Why Do Dogs Jump?

Jumping up on people is one way to get attention, and since dogs do what works, the problem can perpetuate itself to the point where the dog jumps constantly. It is important to understand where jumping comes from and what causes dogs to do this unlikable behavior. Dogs in a pack situation greet each other face to face, and after a few licks and sniffs they have decided whether they are friend or foe and proceed from there to fight or play. When they have been away from their group for a prolonged period of time, they greet each other with a combination of licking and sniffing to re-establish their status within the group and find out where their family members have been.

Dogs that are exuberant greeters need to be taught appropriate manners around guests so that they can be part of family life. After all, jumping works: it gets people to pay attention to them!

⭐ ABOUT FACE!

When pet dogs jump on us, they are trying to get to our faces in order to greet us in a similar manner. This natural behavior, which is actually a gesture of affection and happiness, can easily scare or offend strangers—or owners—resulting in the dog being isolated from the very people she is trying so hard to be with.

The Welcoming Committee

Many people don't like it when their dog jumps on them and place a lot of emphasis on how to stop the behavior of jumping. In truth they are barking up the wrong tree. It is far more effective to define what you prefer the dog to do instead. It is more likely that you will reach your goal if you know what behavior you are looking for so that you can reward your dog for performing the right behavior.

Emphasizing what you want the dog to do by noticing it and rewarding it will help you achieve your goal of a better-mannered pet. Most people choose to have their dogs Sit and Stay when they say hello to people; this is a clear goal for the dog to accomplish and can be used in place of the jumping behavior. You should teach your dog how to Sit and Stay and reinforce it generously when she offers it around people.

Build a History

Rewarding your dog for the right behavior over and over makes the right behavior a more likely choice when your dog is faced with greeting new people. Dogs do what works; if sitting is rewarded when he greets new people, he will try sitting as his first choice. This is where knowing what you want your dog to do comes in handy. If a Sit/Stay is what you want the dog to do instead of jump on guests, then you must reinforce it often and handsomely.

The way to change unwanted behavior is to heavily reinforce appropriate behavior and keep your dog from practicing the wrong behavior as much as possible. For instance, when a guest is visiting, keep a leash on your dog so that you can step on it whenever necessary to prevent your dog from jumping. Click and treat the dog anytime she sits without being asked to. Have the guest go away and try again, but this time, ask for Sit only once. If it happens, click and treat; if it doesn't, the guest goes away. The dog learns by trial and error that if she wants the visitor to stay, she must sit and if she doesn't sit, the guest will leave.

This exercise assumes that you have taught your dog to respond to the Sit command and you have practiced it in all different environments with lots of different types of distractions. Apply the Ten in a Row rule to see if your dog really knows how to Sit in each new environment. Do this by asking your dog to Sit ten times in a row without a click or treat (you can praise each correct repetition). If he doesn't get ten out of ten correct, you have more training to do. Go back to drilling and practicing with him with this distraction until he can pass the test.

Provide Lots of Opportunities to Practice

There is nothing like repetition to aid the learning process. The more opportunities the learner has to practice the desirable behavior and get rewarded for it, the more likely the learner is to offer this new behavior in real life. Making short interesting training sessions—with lots of changes in variables and delicious treats, toys, and games as rewards—will set you on your way to having a dog that knows what to do and does it because you have taught him. Setting up lots of training sessions where you practice different types of greetings will help your dog gain the experience he needs to have good manners anywhere.

Lots of different things are happening when a dog is learning how to greet people without putting his paws on them. Changing these variables slowly enough to maintain the dog's response to the command, yet with enough variation to challenge him a bit, is the key to successful training. Every session will take you that much closer to your goal of a well-mannered pet. Some of the training scenarios for teaching or practicing a polite greeting are:

- A person greeting you and your dog while you are on a walk
- A visitor at the front door
- A person greeting your dog at the pet store or the vet
- A person with a dog greeting you and your dog
- A person sitting and you and your dog approach him
- A person walking up to you while you are sitting with your dog
- A child greeting your dog
- A person with food greeting your dog

The more combinations of variables that you train for, the more reliable your dog will be and the more likely he will be to offer a

Sit/Stay behavior instead of jumping. The key to having things run smoothly is to not change more than one variable at a time. Don't be afraid to go back and review Sit/Stay in places your dog has never been or places where he has a history of jumping and obnoxious behavior. Start off in places where you can get your dog's attention easily, and gradually build up to places that are very distracting for him.

Define Your Dog's Greatest Distraction

Figuring out what makes your dog lose control in different environments will help you break your training sessions down into smaller pieces, making it easier for your dog to be successful. It is important that you do *not* try to train your dog when she is totally out of control, because she isn't thinking about learning or paying attention. It is a more valuable use of your time to take it slow and add in one distraction at a time until your dog learns to ignore all distractions and stay focused on you instead.

Take a minute to think about where you are likely to meet people when you are out on your walk and try to determine the circumstances around her jumping. Does your dog go crazy when she meets new people while you are out for a walk? Are they passing you on the street or approaching you while you are sitting somewhere? What scenario distracts her the most, and what are the circumstances leading up to it? Some of the distractions that dogs find irresistible are: company at your front door, your children coming home from school, your relatives visiting, and people with dogs at the park. Defining the circumstances around which your dog loses control is useful since it gives you an idea of where to start and what you will be working toward.

If your dog is totally out of control around people who come to the door, for instance, you could break down the distraction for your dog into smaller pieces. One of your training sessions could start by practicing Sit and Stay in front of the closed door with no guest; then you could add a family member as the guest; then put the family member outside the door; then add a knock or the door-bell; and eventually build up to being able to practice this with real guests. Breaking the hardest distractions down into small training sessions that introduce one aspect of the distraction at a time is the key for helping your dog to learn a new response in a stimulating environment.

If your dog is more of an outdoor kind of jumper that gets overexcited in play and starts mugging you for the ball, using a leash might help you manage this behavior while you reward him for doing something more appropriate instead. When the dog is excited, ask for Sit once. If he sits, click and throw the ball; if not, tell him "too bad" and walk away for a minute or two and try again after a couple of minutes. The click marks the behavior of sitting on the first try, and the dog's reward is the toss of the ball. What better way to teach your dog some self-control than to make the throwing of the ball dependent upon his response to the Sit command. Once he catches on, even a really energetic dog will love this game. Using games is a great way to enrich your relationship with your dog while fine-tuning his response to basic obedience commands and general control issues.

Avoid Punishing Jumping

Punishment is tempting and seems to work because initially the behavior of jumping goes away. But really, all punishment does is stop the behavior temporarily; it does not instruct the dog to choose the right behavior, nor does it replace jumping with anything but the prediction of being punished. Putting this kind of emphasis on punishment for jumping can backfire with sensitive dogs, making them afraid to greet people and suspicious of hands or knees.

 ABOUT FACE!

Dogs that have aggressive tendencies may actually turn and bite the person who is correcting them, causing a much more serious problem than the one you started with. Remember that punishment comes too late to teach the dog anything, and if poorly timed may teach your dog that visitors mean he's about to get punished.

Instead, set your dog up to do the right thing: Sit instead of jump. Make sure you notice him when he's not jumping and reward him with lots of attention! A wise trainer once said *you get what you pay attention to.* Start paying attention to what's going right and the good stuff will start happening more than you ever imagined.

Remember to Manage the Behavior

Part of every training program to fix behavior problems includes management. Management isn't training so much as it is prevention. You are preventing the dog from practicing a behavior that drives you nuts. Part of managing jumping might involve keeping your dog in another room when guests arrive until you are ready and able to train her.

Even if you only perform minimal management, you should be putting your foot on the dog's leash to prevent her from jumping anytime there are people around. Each time you fail to do this and your dog jumps on someone, you are putting money in the bank for this behavior and it will become stronger with time. Keep a leash by your front door for ready access whenever visitors arrive. Have your foot on your dog's leash anytime you go into the pet store or veterinary office or stop to talk to a neighbor on the street. The fewer opportunities your dog has to jump on people, the more swiftly she will learn to sit instead.

Teaching Sit/Stay with Duration

The duration of a behavior refers to how long the dog has to do the behavior in order to get reinforced. To avoid jumping, you want the dog to Sit and Stay for an extended period of time. You'll want to extend this period of time slowly until your dog will hold the position without trying to jump for one to two minutes. Eventually you'll also want to have your dog perform the Sit/Stay despite the distractions of people or other dogs.

Although you learned how to shape behavior for Sit/Stay, take a moment to review it for these circumstances:

1. Use a treat to lure her nose upward and move your hand slightly back.
2. When her bottom hits the floor, click and treat.

3. Repeat this until your dog is offering Sit readily when she sees your hand above her head.

4. Practice without the treat in your hand. Click when her bottom hits the floor and follow up with a treat.

5. Put the treats off your person and repeat, running with the dog to go get the treat after you click for her bottom hitting the ground.

6. Introduce distractions or train somewhere new and go back to the beginning if necessary.

7. Change the variables to mimic the ones that happen in real life: people visiting at the park, on the street, at the pet store, as well as at home.

8. Build duration in a nondistracting environment and increase it to double the amount of time you'll think you need. To build duration, simply count extra seconds between clicks and treats until your dog is easily waiting twenty to forty seconds for her click and treat.

Building in a long duration for Sit/Stay will help you in public when there are distractions. In practice you may be working on thirty seconds and in real life your dog may give you only fifteen seconds, but it's a start. Even fifteen seconds will give you time to react quickly enough to keep your dog from putting her paws on a visitor.

Creating a Sitting Maniac

It isn't hard to get a dog hooked on a behavior that works, but it does take time and thought along the way. One great activity to keep things interesting for puppies is the Sit for a Treat game. To play this game in a group-dog setting, take your dog off his leash and wander around the room greeting other puppies. Approach one of the other puppies with your dog and have the owner of that puppy ask her dog to Sit, asking only once. If the pup sits on the first try, click and treat and move on to the next dog. If the puppy doesn't sit on the first try, simply walk away and ignore the pup, moving on to the next one. Sometimes if the puppies are very high energy it takes awhile for them to catch on, but pretty soon several pups will be sitting perfectly in the middle of the room while the rest are running all willy-nilly around them. One or two lone pups may be sitting stoically, refusing to move for anything—they know exactly what they need to do to get people to pay attention to them.

Play this game at home by inviting a bunch of family or friends over and doing the same exercise. Have everyone wander around, armed with clickers and treats, and take turns giving only one command to Sit and clicking and treating your dog for responding on the first try. Pretty soon, you will see your dog going from person to person, sitting as fast as his rear end will let him to earn his goody. Use your dog's dinner for this exercise if you'd like; it's a great way for him to practice his good manners and earn his dinner doing it.

Jumping is a natural behavior gone astray through inappropriate reinforcement of the wrong behavior. There is nothing difficult about teaching your dog to Sit instead of jump, it just needs to be practiced in increasingly distracting environments until your dog adopts it as second nature. Remember, as with any bad habit or addiction (yes, some dogs are so good at jumping that they have become addicted to it), it takes time and patience to change unwanted behavior. Through lots of repetitions and opportunities to practice the right behavior you will find that your dog will be sitting for attention instead of mugging people. Owning a dog that knows how to greet guests politely makes it easier to take your dog anywhere and have him actively involved in your life.

CHAPTER 6

Going AWOL: Outdoor Problems

Outdoor problems are tough with a new recruit, because the outside world is so exciting for a young private. The trick is to be understanding yet firm.

If there is a common problem among dogs, it is pulling on the leash to get to where they want to go. From the biggest Great Dane to the tiniest Chihuahua, all dogs regardless of their size learn to pull on their leashes from an early age.

The Only Solution Is Training

Leash pulling doesn't seem to be such a big problem until you try to walk around the block with a dog that thinks she's the lead dog in a sled team, determined to reach the dog park in record time. Pulling on the leash is one of the major reasons people stop taking their dogs for walks—it takes all the fun out of a leisurely walk around the neighborhood when one of your arms feels as though it is being pulled out of its socket.

If you look in pet stores and in pet supply catalogs, you will see dozens of devices that supposedly magically stop your dog from pulling. The truth of the matter, however, is that dogs will continue to pull until you teach them to stop, regardless of the equipment you are using. Only you, as your dog's trusted companion, can choose what method you want to use to teach your dog to walk with you instead of drag you, and there are many options out there that you can try.

The key to any training program, however, is *you*—how much time you invest in the project and how consistent you are about sticking to it until the job is done.

Define Your Terms

Whenever you want to fix any behavior problem, it is a good idea to sit down and figure out what you would like your dog to do instead. In this case, it is important to define how you want your dog to behave on leash. Do you want her to walk at perfect heel position or is a loose leash sufficient? Where exactly would you like your dog to be, and what will it look like when she's there? Will your arm be relaxed or extended, is sniffing okay, and which side should she be on?

Narrowing down what you are looking for gives you a better idea of what you are going to reinforce and will help you recognize it and reward it. Only by reinforcing the right behavior will you be able to get rid of the undesirable one. If you don't know what your dog has to do to get the reward, you will not be successful at getting rid of pulling and teaching him an acceptable alternative. Sit down with your family now and decide how you want your dog to behave on leash.

Lack of Exercise Contribution

Nowhere is a lack of exercise more apparent than when a dog is on leash. A dog with few outlets for his energy will pull, spin, and tug on leash to get where he wants to go. Giving your dog appropriate outlets for his energy, such as playing with other dogs, swimming, and playing fetch, will help give you a more calm on-leash companion. Active dogs need at least thirty minutes to an hour a day of flat-out running to take the edge off of their energy. Without this outlet you can expect behavior problems. Exercise is part of a dog's basic needs for mental, physical, and emotional stability and to ignore this fact is to set your dog up for failure. If you don't have the time to exercise your dog to the point of fatigue, consider hiring a pet sitter, dog walker, or doggie day care professional to help you. Trying to train a dog that is not getting enough exercise is a project in frustration and should be avoided at all costs.

Walk Without Pulling

Teaching your dog to walk at your side rather than pull your arm off requires lots of practice and repetition. This is not a behavior that is going to change overnight. Remember that pulling works, or has worked, for quite a long time for most dogs, and behavior that gets reinforced gets repeated.

 ABOUT FACE!

A huge step in the right direction is to stop following the dog when the leash is tight and she's pulling you. This may mean suspending all walks around the block so that she doesn't have the opportunity to practice pulling.

Managing your dog's behavior by not allowing her to practice it isn't teaching her to walk next to you, but it's a step in the right direction since she isn't being reinforced for the wrong behavior. Following are some tips for teaching loose-leash walking:

- Walk at a brisk pace and change direction frequently so that your dog has to pay attention to where you are going. The more turns you offer, the more your dog has to pay attention to where you are.
- Once you get the hang of walking and turning frequently, start to pay attention to the moment your dog turns to follow you, and click and treat him for catching up to you.
- At first, you may want to stop walking for a moment after the click so that the dog realizes what exactly he's getting clicked for. Use really delicious treats that your dog loves to keep his attention focused on you.
- Start off practicing in a distraction-free place, and gradually go to busier places when your dog starts to understand what you want.
- Attaching a six-foot leash to your waist will keep your hands free for this exercise, so you will be able to click and treat your dog when he is next to you. Remember that the message you are sending to your dog is that pulling does not get him where he wants to go because when he pulls in one direction it makes you go the other way.
- For most dogs, the faster you walk the better, since a steady pace forces them to pay attention to where you are going next.

- Using a clicker to mark the behavior of being next to you will shorten your training time by half. The clicker tells the dog exactly what he's doing right to earn the reward. The clicker is clearer and more precise than any other tool you can use.

When you want to change a behavior that has been working for the dog for quite some time, you need to reinforce the right behavior often and with a high-value reward. Your dog has been pulling to get where she's going for as long as you've had her, so in order to get rid of pulling you must replace it with a behavior she finds more rewarding. In order for her to choose to walk next to you over pulling, you will have to do lots of repetitions with yummy rewards.

Really great reinforcements can take the shape of treats like cheese, freeze-dried liver, roast beef, or chicken, or favorite games like tug or fetch. Whatever the reward, the dog has to want it more than she wants to pull. Be creative and fun and your dog will soon be trotting happily next to you.

Adding Duration to Your Walks

From a training standpoint, duration refers to the amount of time your dog can maintain the requested behavior. In this case, it's the length of time that the dog has to be next to you in order to earn his click and treat. Once your dog starts to catch on to getting clicked for coming back to your side, you can then raise the criteria to his coming back to your side and staying there for a step or two. Eventually you will build the length of time the dog must walk next to you to several minutes, until the dog no longer wants to pull. Remember, duration refers to the length of time the dog must do the behavior before he gets rewarded. Practice having him walk with you for different lengths of time around a variety of distractions until he can trot happily next to you under any circumstance.

Changing the Variables and Distractions

Practicing in a new environment—with people, dogs, cars, bicycles, and other distractions—is critical to the reliability of the behavior. Changing too many of these variables at once, however, will make your dog's behavior of walking next to you fall apart. To help your dog to learn to stay with you despite the distractions, change one variable at a time. The variables involved in heeling refer to how close or far you are to the distractions and how intense the distractions are (one person, a crowd, kids, adults, people with dogs, wildlife, cars, bikes, and so forth).

By controlling the variables and working slowly to introduce distractions while you maintain your dog's ability to walk at heel, you will teach your dog to walk nicely on a leash regardless of the distractions in the environment. Don't ever be afraid to stop the training session and make it easier for the dog to be right if things are going badly and your dog could use some extra help.

Controlling Heeling

There are two major variables involved in teaching your dog to heel: the distance to the distraction and the intensity of the distraction. The distance between your dog and the distraction is too close if you can't get the dog to perform the behavior. If this is the case you should back away from the action to a point where your dog will perform the behavior well. Once your dog is working well, you can decrease the distance between your dog and the distraction, bringing her closer to the action when you are sure your dog can handle it.

Setting your dog up for success is key to becoming a good dog trainer. Here are ways that you can set your dog up for success.

- Reduce the intensity of the distraction (quieter, slower, less of it) as needed.
- Use treats; training is difficult, so make it worth his while.
- Offer a high rate of reinforcement in a new environment.
- Slow the rate down (click and treat less frequently) for longer versions of the behavior (dog stays with you longer), and when the dog starts to be able to perform the behavior reliably.

Choose what distraction you will start with and set it up so that your dog can be successful. The intensity of the distraction has to do with its speed, noise level, and quantity. The intensity is too high when your dog can't perform the behavior because he is too distracted. The solution to this problem is to tone down the distraction by making it go slower, quieter, or having less of it.

Common Distractions

Another consideration when you are working your dog around distractions is the type of distraction you are working on. There are three major categories of distractions, things that move, things that smell, and things that make noise.

1. **Things that move.** This category incites your dog's prey drive, her desire to chase after things that move. Every dog has a different level of distractibility, but most dogs find things that move irresistible. Examples include cars, squirrels, runners, dogs, motorcycles, balls, or kids.

2. **Things that smell.** The majority of dogs are motivated most by their stomachs, so for the hunting breeds especially, the "nose to the ground" behavior can be quite a challenge. Examples are food, animals, other animals' feces, and wildlife.

3. **Things that make noise.** Some dogs are more sensitive to sound than others. The average dog that is simply curious will get over it quickly and learn to ignore sounds if you change the variables, distance, and intensity slowly.

Distractions need to be worked into the training gradually. If distractions are too frequent or intense, the dog will get overexcited and be unable to concentrate, and no real learning will occur. It is important that you pay attention to his excitement level and tone down the distractions so that he is able to absorb the lesson.

The Mule Impersonator

Laggards often plant their butts and will not move forward. They will not move or follow you with any amount of coaxing or cooing. There are several tricks you can use to get these dogs to follow you:

1. Put tension in the lead but don't pull. Make sure the leash is hooked to a regular collar, not a training collar.
2. As soon as your dog takes a step toward you to steady herself, be ready to click and treat and lavish with praise (some dogs take a while, so be patient).
3. Repeat this every time your dog stops. Don't go back to her; simply ignore the wrong behavior and pay attention to the right one instead.
4. Within ten minutes or so most dogs give up their stubborn-mule impression and go with you. Some dogs may need you to do this over several sessions before they give up.

Use Grand Rewards

Teaching your dog to heel can be time consuming and boring—for both of you—if you don't come up with ideas to make it more interesting and fun. One way to make things more fun is to hide the rewards all around your training area before you start your session. It will be such a surprise to the dog to be rewarded with a delicious treat or an awesome toy that she wasn't expecting to be pulled out of the bushes. The element of surprise will make you far more interesting to your dog, and it will make your dog much more willing to learn to walk with you.

You may also want to consider using a variety of rewards paired with the click. Some examples are a game of tug, a game of fetch, a stuffed toy, a fantastic belly or flank rub, and lots of excited praise. You can teach your dog that you are interesting and full of great surprises by hiding your goodies everywhere and keeping your dog guessing about what you're going to pull out next.

Training Equipment

Training collars, head halters, and other devices are just that: devices. Their purpose is to manage pulling while you are teaching your dog to heel. The goal should be to have your dog learn to heel with the help of a training device and then to wean the dog off that device and have her heel without it.

Collars and Leashes

You can find several training devices that keep dogs from pulling. The most common are the regular slip collar or choke chain, the pinch collar, and the head halter. The slip collar works by restricting the dog's airway for a fraction of a second and making it unpleasant for him to pull. The pinch collar works by pinching the skin around the dog's neck and making it unpleasant to pull. The head halter works by pulling the dog's head downward, making it impossible to walk until the dog stops pulling and walks closer to the handler.

As with any device, you must teach your dog the step-by-step process for heeling, and in most cases this should occur before you start using the device itself. After the dog has learned how to get rewarded, the use of a training device will help you sort out the various distractions. Special situations, such as the veterinary clinic, may require extra management before your dog is completely trained. No one device is right for every dog, but the head halter is probably the most useful for most dogs.

Head-Halter Benefits

There is one particular name brand of head halter, the Gentle Leader Headcollar, which tends to fit better than others available on the market today. It has two adjustable straps: one for the neck and one for the muzzle. The leash clips underneath the dog's chin. Think of the way a halter on a horse fits and you'll have an idea of how this works. The principle behind why the head halter is superior to other training devices is that it controls the dog's forward movement by controlling the dog's head. You would never expect to move a horse by pulling on its neck for instance, but you can easily move a 1,200-pound animal in the direction you want to go by guiding it by its head—well, at least most of the time!

This same principle works for dogs. The head halter is not a muzzle—the dog can still eat, catch a ball, and bite with it on, and no dog should be left unattended while wearing it. If your dog should try to bite or eat something he shouldn't while wearing it, you can close his mouth by gently pulling up on the leash. The pressure that the head halter exerts will close his mouth and pull his head down, effectively preventing him from continuing the behavior. The head halter is sometimes described as self-correcting, meaning the handler does not have to pull on the leash or yank the dog in any way to get him to stop what he is doing. It is also important to note that if you choose to use this device, you should attach only a six-foot leash to it, never an extendable or retractable one. If your dog were to take off after something and hit the end of a long leash while wearing a head halter, he could injure his neck. Introduce the head halter over a period of about two weeks. The longer you take to make this fun for the dog, the more useful a training tool it will be.

The introduction of the head halter should be a gradual process, whereby you slowly teach the dog that wearing it is fun and means good stuff is about to happen. Make him as excited to see the head halter as he is to see his leash. Using a clicker and the yummiest treats, introduce the head halter by following these steps:

1. Show the halter to your dog and click and treat her for sniffing at it.

2. Open the nose loop and click and treat your dog for poking her nose through it to get at the treat.

3. Once she's eagerly putting her nose through the loop on her own, give her a good-sized treat and while she's chewing, fasten the neck strap.

4. Let her move around a bit and click and treat her for not pawing at her nose.

5. If your dog gets the nose loop off, take the whole thing off and leave her alone for ten minutes or so. Completely ignoring her will make her all the more eager to work with you again. The idea here is that she will want to keep the halter on because you pay extra attention to her and give special treats only when she has it on.

6. Later, when she isn't pawing as much, attach a leash to the clip under the chin and repeat steps 4 and 5. You will have

to go back and click and treat her for walking without pawing at her face every time you introduce a new distraction.

7. You are now ready to use the head halter on your walks, but go slowly. Take your dog for a short walk, and click and treat her for walking outside without pawing at her face. Keep the walk to no more than five minutes long.

8. As your dog gets used to wearing the head halter in public, you can gradually increase the distractions, the length of time you walk her, and any of the other variables.

Remember to make it easy for the dog to be right if you notice any regression around distractions. This is especially common when other dogs are present. The head halter can be a wonderful tool for helping you manage your dog around distractions and teaching her not to pull, but introducing it takes time. If this device isn't useful for a dog, it is usually because the owner rushed the introduction because the dog seemed to tolerate it fairly well. Don't be fooled—just like with training other things, you get out what you put in. The following are tips for making this work for you.

- Be patient during this introduction. The head halter is a more useful tool if you introduce it slowly and let the dog learn to like wearing it (up to a week or two).
- You will have no need for jerks or pops or corrections with a head halter; in fact, doing so can injure a dog's neck or spine.
- Lunging or pulling can injure your dog's neck or spine, causing him discomfort and long-term medical problems.

- Make sure you read the halter's directions carefully before you use it on your dog. It's important that you teach your dog to wear it and avoid letting him lunge or pull while wearing it.
- If you have trouble, find a qualified positive trainer to help you introduce this piece of equipment to your dog.

Teaching your dog to walk without pulling definitely is a time-consuming task, but it is well worth the effort. Having a dog that will walk politely beside you without yanking your arm off makes him a more pleasant companion that you won't mind taking anywhere with you. Remember that you need to build your dog's bank account for not pulling through lots of practice and consistency. At the very least, stop letting him practice the behavior of pulling by stopping every time he hits the end of the leash. By using the right equipment, introducing distractions slowly, and controlling the distance, you will gradually teach your canine companion that walking with you, rather than dragging you, is the better alternative.

Going AWOL

Recruits that don't come when they are called have learned that getting away from you is rewardable. If they run off and find things to eat, roll in, and play with, then running away has huge benefits and it doesn't give them much incentive to come and be with you.

Why Do Dogs Run Away?

When the average person calls her dog, she puts the leash back on and goes home, or crates the dog and goes to work, or puts the dog in the car and drives away. Since it normally isn't beneficial for the dog to come to his owner, because his owner doesn't provide a very rewarding consequence, the dog chooses to reward himself and run away.

The difference between a trained dog that comes when called and an untrained dog that doesn't is based on the dog's perception of who controls what he wants. Dogs behave in ways that benefit them, so the key to having a dog that is willing to come when called is making it worth the dog's while, regardless of the distraction. Trained dogs know that their owners hold the keys to everything they want, and the rule is that the dog must do something to get it.

Use a Leash to Control the Variables

The most important thing to remember is that every time your dog takes off and has a good time she is putting money in her bank account for not coming back. Don't allow an untrained dog off leash in an unsafe area or an area where she will be difficult to catch.

✪ ABOUT FACE!

When you eventually get to the point where you are not using a leash anymore, it will be easy to get rid of it and still have the same level of behavior. Since you have not used the leash to teach her to come by yanking on it, but instead used it to merely limit her options, you have made it more likely that she will choose you over the distraction.

A dog that has an unreliable recall is a danger to herself. She doesn't have good judgment and will often run in the street, get lost, or eat something harmful. If you love your dog, use a leash in unfenced areas so that you do not give your dog the opportunity to run away.

Keeping your dog on leash gives her the ability to be right more often and allows you to reinforce those choices, making it likely she will choose you again and again.

Make Sure the Rewards Are Worth the Effort
Your dog needs you to use the best possible rewards if he's going to choose coming to you over pursuing a distraction. Remember that a squirrel, cat, child, or another dog is a thrill to chase, bark at, or sniff around. If your dog chooses to be with you over the distraction, make sure you have the best treats, toys, or games as the reward. You will mark your dog's behavior of turning in your direction with a click and follow it by a treat, a game, or an opportunity to interact with the distraction (but only after checking in with you first). Using rewards in this way is not a bribe; you are simply requiring that your dog check in with you before he gets what he wants. For dogs that learn this game, it almost completely eliminates the desire to run away. Using rewards in this way means you control the dog's access to what he wants and you pay up when he checks in with you.

Ideas for Rewards
Making the rewards variable and exciting will enhance your dog's performance and make the process of teaching your dog to come all the more fun. Here are some things to keep in mind

when you are considering different types of rewards in your training program.

- Food rewards can include cheese, liver, chicken, beef jerky, tortellini, hot dogs, roast beef, and steak.
- Toy rewards can include stuffed animals, balls, tug toys, Frisbees, etc.
- Games rewards like fetch, tug, and Frisbee can help a high-energy dog stay focused on you and redirect the energy that would have been used to chase the distraction.
- Real-life rewards include the opportunity to chase the distraction (a ball, a squirrel, a leaf), to go say hello to the person or other dog, to go play with the group of dogs off leash nearby, to go swim in the pond, go plow through the snow, roll in the smell, or whatever.

Leadership Matters

Ninety percent of a dog's recall has to do with who's in charge. Dogs with firm, strong leaders almost always come when called because you are in charge of everything great and your judgment is worth trusting. Being a leader does in no way imply being a bully or making your dog do something; in fact, true leaders never have to force a dog to do anything. Leadership is about setting limits and having rules about what is allowed and what is not allowed. Having guidelines is essential if your dog is going to do as you wish.

Being the leader means that you control the resources that the dog wants. It does not mean, under any circumstances, that you dominate or bully the dog in any way. Here are some guidelines for you to review:

1. Nothing in life is free. Your dog must do something to get something.
2. Respond quickly to commands. Pick a number of seconds that you'll give your dog to respond; if he doesn't respond on the first command within the time frame you've chosen, he doesn't get whatever you were about to give him.
3. No dogs on your bed. No dog, let alone a dog with a behavior problem (especially a recall problem), should be allowed to sleep on the highest, most privileged spot in the house: your bed.
4. Leaders go first through doorways and up and down stairs. Teach your dog to wait and let you go first.
5. No dogs on the furniture; your dog should be on the floor or in her crate or bed.
6. Leaders control space and move about without interference. Don't step over or around your dog; if he's in your way, make him move.
7. Leaders initiate attention and games. Pushy dogs that hound you with toys or nudging should be ignored until they give up. You can call them to you later when it's your idea to play.

You, as the leader, can control what your dog wants by controlling his options and what he's allowed to have. The rule is that when you are experiencing behavior problems you need to be strict about allowing privileges and having house rules. When your dog behaves in a more acceptable way in a few months' time, you can relax some of the rules here and there without losing your status as leader. Think of it as similar to allowing a child to stay up later in the summertime. Staying up later in the summer is a special thing for a child; once September comes, she knows she will have to go to bed at the usual time.

Building a Foundation for Come

The foundation for Come is the most important part of the exercise. It requires that your dog turn away from the distraction and look back at you (and eventually move toward you as well). The Come command is really a Leave It command, because the dog has to turn away from what it wants and come back to you. The more reliable your dog is about turning away from the things it wants, the better able you will be to get her to come to you anytime, anyplace. If you teach a strong foundation for self-control, Come will be easier to train, and your dog will be reliable anywhere you take her. Although you have already taught Come, take a moment to review the shaping steps again:

1. Stand with your dog on a leash and don't let her get to what she wants; when your dog turns away from what she wants and looks back at you, click and treat.
2. If it takes your dog more than a minute to look back, you are too close to the distraction; back away.

3. When the dog is turning in your direction easily, run backwards as she turns to look at you and let her catch you. Click your dog as she is moving toward you and put the treat at your feet.

4. Practice putting the treat between your feet, so when he takes it, it will be easier for you to catch him.

5. Practice handling your dog's collar and leading her by it, clicking and treating her for tolerating being led by it.

6. Label the behavior Come when you have the dog by the collar.

7. Change the environment and distractions, practicing in various places.

8. Use a longer leash, twelve to twenty-five feet, and repeat from the beginning.

9. Let your leash drag until your dog proves she understands the command.

10. Vary the size and type of rewards to keep the dog guessing as to what she'll get as a reward.

Change Old Patterns

Old habits die hard, and a dog that consistently runs away to entertain itself is practicing the very opposite of the behavior you are trying to teach her. If your dog has run away a lot in the past and gotten away with rewarding itself again and again, you are going to have to put in a lot of time to prevent her from running away and reward her for coming with really memorable rewards. Some dogs refuse to come to you because nothing good happens when they do. For instance, just before you leave for work, you call your dog in from the yard, put him in his crate, and leave him there for eight hours. Or at the park, you call him away from his dog friends and then put him in the car and go home.

ABOUT FACE!

Try to change this setup by calling him several times before you actually need to leave and allow him to go back to playing as the reward. Changing your pattern of behavior (calling the dog and putting him back on leash, for instance) may be harder than you think.

Again, having a plan of action—what you desire and what you will reward—will make training easier. Prepare ahead of time how you are going to react, and you will be rewarded by a dog that is much more likely to come to you than run away and reward itself.

Keep Recall Positive

Punishment only stops the undesirable behavior, it doesn't teach the dog anything. By the time you've punished your dog for running away, you have him back. In his mind, you are punishing him for coming to you, making it unlikely that you'll get him to respond enthusiastically in the future.

Remote punishment through the use of electronic collars is also not appropriate in the hands of the average pet owner. Even when used by professionals, such devices can teach the dog to be distrustful and fearful of her environment. It is much safer and more reasonable to teach your dog what you expect of her and avoid punishment altogether. When it comes right down to it, punishment misses the point; it is almost always issued too late to be instructive and if it isn't delivered with perfect timing, it will have absolutely no positive effect on the dog's behavior. Use your time and energy wisely—teach the dog what is expected of her instead of punishing her for making a mistake.

Safe Confinement

You can confine your dog any number of ways, but it's important to pay careful attention to details so that she can't escape. Keep in mind that no dog should be left unsupervised outdoors unless you have an absolutely escape-proof, locked, chain-link run. You can call a fence company to come and design a dog pen to fit your needs, but keep in mind that dogs that are confined outdoors tend to develop barking problems.

If you build your own pen, you must keep several things in mind during design and construction. Ideally, you should bury ¼-inch mesh wire about three to four inches under a gravel base; that way if your dog decides to dig, she can't dig out. Watch your dog carefully to make sure she doesn't eat the gravel. There are several options you can consider for the bottom surface of the pen. A cement slab may be a good choice if there is adequate shade, but it is not the most comfortable surface to lie on in extreme weather conditions (either hot or cold). One very effective solution is concrete patio block (or pavers) surrounded by crushed stone. The size of the stone can be whatever you feel would be best for your dog.

Depending on the size of your dog pen, you could put some kind of doghouse or shelter at one end, use patio block for half the length, and leave the rest just plain stone. This arrangement makes it easier to disinfect the pen, keeps the smell to a minimum, and is attractive to look at. A locked gate is essential to prevent anyone from stealing your dog. It is really not a good idea to leave your dog unattended, but in circumstances where you need to be gone for an extended period, a pen will at least give your dog a chance to relieve himself in an appropriate place.

Invisible Fences

An invisible fence is a buried wire around the perimeter of your property provides an electrical barrier that prevents your dog from leaving your yard. To keep your dog within the confines of the yard, your dog wears a collar that gives it an electrical correction if it crosses the barrier. The biggest problem with these fences is that they do not prevent people or animals from coming onto your property, which is why you should never leave your dog unsupervised in an invisibly fenced area.

Invisible fencing lets you restrict your dog's access to certain areas, like swimming pools, driveways, or decorative gardens. In order for this kind of fencing to be used humanely, your dog must be taught to respect the barrier. Hire a qualified professional dog trainer to help you teach your dog where the boundaries are and how to avoid getting corrected.

Although this book promotes positive training methods, if someone can't afford to fence their yard properly, an invisible fence is much better than doing nothing. Not using preventative measures increases the risk of the dog getting lost or killed. Keep in mind that some dogs are not bothered by the electrical correction and will run through it. A physical barrier in the form of chain link or solid wood is a better choice for dogs like these.

Front-Door Safety

Making sure your dog doesn't slip out the front door is essential to keeping her safe. Try to prevent front-door escapes by thinking ahead and perhaps denying access to the door through which your dog is most likely to escape. Tighten your screen door so that it closes more quickly, or put a baby gate that locks in the doorway to prevent escapes. Teach your children to be mindful of where the dog is when they are coming and going.

 **ABOUT FACE!**

Put your dog in a crate or gated room when there are a lot of kids and adults coming and going. Family parties and holiday gatherings are notorious times for dogs to escape and get hit by cars. When you have less control of the home environment, pay special attention to your dog's environment; prevention is half the cure.

Spend some time teaching your dog appropriate door manners, like sitting and staying without going through the door (even if it's wide open) until told to do so. This requires lots of on-leash setups with a helper to hold the leash in case your dog tries to make a break. You'll want to practice at first with the door shut and then gradually build up to your dog holding the Stay while you open and close the door. You can even increase the difficulty by actually going through the door and leaving the dog in a Stay. The key point to remember here is to reinforce the dog for holding the Stay, not coming through the door. Make sure you practice often and provide a high rate of reinforcement for the right behavior.

A Last Word About the Outdoors: Digging

So, your recruit is in her pen in the yard, safe from busy roads and in her own barracks. Everything is okay, right? Wrong. You go outside to see your puppy has turned your yard into a minefield of holes, and she happily lumbers over to you covered with dirt.

Digging is practically the only problem that cannot be prevented, lessened, or solved with obedience training (although sometimes training, because it relieves boredom, indirectly reduces the behavior).

 ABOUT FACE!

Dogs don't dig because they are dominant, belligerent, unaware of authority, or out of control—they do it instinctually to make a cool or warm place to lie down or to make a nestlike den for their puppies. And, yes, interesting smells in the soil, the wonderful feeling of vigorous burrowing, and dirt in their toes are hard for any dog to resist.

Monitoring your dog and correcting digging attempts is an ongoing process—you aren't fighting your dog, you are fighting nature. Your best option is to never leave your dog unsupervised in an area with digging potential, but if you can't always do that. The best thing to do is recognize and accept your dog's need to dig, and then give him a place where he can do it to his heart's content. Choose a part of your yard or garden that can be your puppy's sandbox, just as you'd provide for a child. Make sure the area is large enough and block it off with a border. Dig a small hole in the spot and put a cheese-smeared bone in it. Bring your dog over, and when he starts digging in the spot, praise him. If he gets rewarded for digging here, he'll probably return to check it out again. Refresh the goodies you stash in this spot occasionally.

Another option is to exercise him vigorously and regularly so he doesn't seek aerobic activity from digging. For some dogs that's still not enough. If you live near a beach or a park or someplace where digging won't permanently deface the landscape, encourage your dog to dig there. Fill previously dug holes with dog feces. Most won't return to dig in that hole—especially if they're finding tasty treats by digging somewhere else.

CHAPTER 7

Fire in the Hole: Housebreaking

The first thing every new drill sergeant should know before bringing a recruited puppy into the house is that the puppy needs to know where the outhouse is, or, where he can relieve himself. The good news is that all puppies can be housetrained. The bad news is that a puppy rarely becomes housetrained by just letting him out several times a day.

The Basics of Housetraining

This comprehensive housetraining plan requires dedication—but it's simple and foolproof. Just keep up with your puppy's training! Here are some simple rules to follow:

- Confine your puppy to his crate when you can't watch him so he won't relieve himself where he's not supposed to or while you're not looking (if you prefer, use a baby gate to confine him to the kitchen or laundry room while you can't watch him—just make sure the room is puppy-proofed).
- Supervise your puppy when he is out of his crate.

- Feed him a high-quality diet at scheduled times and try to limit treats.
- Take him to his potty spot as soon as you return home, soon after meals, and when he wakes up from a nap.
- Teach him to eliminate on command by saying "Go potty, good puppy" in an excited voice while he's doing his business.
- Clean up his accidents immediately (remove debris or moisture, then treat with neutralizer and cleaner).
- Never correct him after the fact.
- Keep a log of his habits (when and where he pooped or peed, and when and how much he ate and drank).

Crate Training

Until a puppy is perfectly trained, he needs a safe place in which he can do nothing wrong. So when you can't keep your eyes glued to your puppy and monitor his every move, confine him to a place where inappropriate behavior—soiling, stealing, shredding, chewing, or scratching—isn't an option. I suggest crating because it eliminates the risk of him damaging woodwork, flooring, wall covering, or cabinetry.

Assuming you ultimately want your puppy to enjoy freedom in the house, crating is almost a rearing necessity. Crating is widely accepted by behaviorists, puppy trainers, veterinarians, and knowledgeable puppy owners as a humane means of confinement. Provided your puppy is properly introduced, you should feel as comfortable about crating him in your absence as you would securing a toddler in a highchair at mealtime.

Whether the enclosure is a room, hallway, kennel, or crate, it should be:

- **The right size.** It should be large enough that when your puppy is a full-grown dog he'll be able to stand without his shoulders touching the ceiling of the crate. This sized crate will be far too large for your puppy at first. Use a divider to limit the amount of space your puppy has; for the first month or so, one-third to one-half the crate should be fine.
- **Safe.** Homemade enclosures may save you money, but you would feel awful if he poked himself in the eye, stabbed or hung himself, or swallowed wood splinters or material like wallpaper or blankets because you ignored potential dangers. Make sure there are no protrusions or sharp edges, and no ingestible components.
- **Puppy-proof.** If he is prone to chewing, scratching or jumping up, prevent access to any woodwork, linoleum, furniture, counters, garbage, or windows so your home doesn't become a victim of your puppy's destructiveness during his training period.

Introducing Puppy to His Bunk

Though your puppy will come to think of his crate as his sanctuary because it satisfies a puppy's denning instinct, he may not like the idea of going in the crate at first. If you reinforce his objections to the crate by making his early associations with it unpleasant, he may never adjust to it. And that will be a setback for both of you. Go slowly, and praise every positive step along the way.

Line the bottom of the crate with newspaper for extra insulation from the cold floor, then put a soft blanket or piece of fleece on top of the newspaper. Hopefully your puppy will never eliminate on his sleeping material in his crate, but don't bet on it, especially not in the first few weeks. The blanket or fleece should be machine washable, and of course the newspapers can be thrown away.

⊙ ABOUT FACE!

Make the crate a safe and cozy place for your puppy. Put it somewhere your pup will have privacy, but not where he'll feel alone. A corner of the kitchen is usually a good spot. Soon your pup will love going in there and relaxing!

Get your puppy into a good chew toy habit right away by putting an appropriate chew toy in the crate. Puppies need to chew, so unless you want them to go to work on your shoes, furniture, floor—whatever—turn them on to puppy-appropriate toys early.

When his crate looks like something you might want to curl up and nap in, call him over to it. Let him sniff it. Don't push him toward it or into it. Let him discover it in his own time. Make it interesting for him by putting some small bits of something really tasty like cold cuts or cheese near the entrance. When he shows interest, toss a goody into the crate. If he runs in and gobbles it up, tell him what a good puppy he is.

Don't shut the door on him the first time he goes in the crate. Let him go in and out a few times, continuing to praise when he shows interest. After all this stimulation, take him to his potty spot. This is his first introduction to the crate.

Later, feed your puppy in the crate. Place him and his food inside and sit with your back blocking the doorway of the crate. Don't close the crate door. For his next meal, prop the crate door and sit at the opening with your puppy. Keeping his food in the bowl, place a few pieces of kibble in the crate, then feed him a few pieces from your hand outside the crate. This way he associates being fed as something that happens in the crate and out. Feeding your puppy from your hands is also an excellent way to teach him that your hands mean good things. Your puppy (and later, your dog) should always associate your hands (and any person's hands) coming toward him as a good thing. There may be times when you have to grab his collar or take his food away or when strangers want to pet him.

Going to Bed

Next, teach your puppy to enter and exit the crate on command. Put his paws right in front of the opening. With one hand on his collar and the other pointing into the crate, say, "Bed." Gently guide him in by the collar as you place your hand under his tail and behind his rear legs to prevent him from backing away. If necessary, gently lift him in. Immediately invite him out by saying, "Okay," and praising him for coming out to you.

Practice several repetitions of this routine—without being enclosed. If you shut him in and leave him every time he is put in the enclosure he may develop a bad association with crating. But when he learns to go in the crate on command as a result of frequent practice, he is more likely to also accept being enclosed.

If you reserve his favorite toy for the times he spends in the crate, he may actually look forward to crating as an opportunity to play with it. Leave food and water out of the crate; puppies don't need it in there and most likely they will dump or scatter it instead of eating or drinking. Create a peaceful environment by covering the crate with a sheet or, if his tendency is to pull it in, surround the crate with a couple of stiff panels for a more enclosed, den-like atmosphere.

What to Do If Puppy Barks in the Crate

Sometimes a puppy will bark, yodel, whine, or howl when crated. Unless he is trying to tell you he has to go potty, ignore any noise he might make. Most pups will quiet down if you ignore their pleas. If yours doesn't and you or your family members are losing sleep or sanity, startle him into being quiet, use a word for it ("Shush") and praise for the quietness.

To startle your barking or crying puppy, your timing has to be good. While he's in full voice, throw an empty soda can at his covered crate or clap your hands sharply twice. You can also create an earthquake by attaching the leash to his crate and giving it a quick jerk as he barks.

Do these things where your puppy can't see you. You don't want him to associate you with things that startle or scare him. As soon as he's quiet, come in and say, "Shush." If he stays quiet, say, "Good Shush" very enthusiastically. You may need to do this a number of times before he learns what Shush means. He'll still try to get your attention by barking or crying. Combine ignoring the noise and startling him until he figures out that you only praise him when he's settled down.

⊗ ABOUT FACE!

A crate-trained puppy is not housetrained. Your puppy is likely to do things you're not going to like when loose in the house and, therefore, needs plenty of supervised exploration to learn the house rules. If your puppy is out of his crate, keep your eyes glued on him or, better still, umbilical-cord him so when you can't follow him, he'll follow you; this affords you the opportunity to curtail misbehaviors before they become habits.

Umbilical cording was addressed earlier in the book, then as just keeping your puppy on a leash in the house. There is another version of this, and here's how it works: Tie his leash to your belt on your left side. Give him only enough slack to keep him at your side without your legs becoming entangled. If he attempts to jump up, chew, bark, or relieve himself without your approval, you'll be able to stop him instantly by tugging on the lead to distract him. You'll also be able to tell him what a good puppy he is when he trots after you or sits by your side as you work around the house or sit down to do something. Umbilical-cording is a fantastically simple technique and important training tool, which every able-bodied household member should use. You can even umbilical-cord two puppies at once. Or when one pet is trained and the other isn't, you can cord the untrained puppy while giving the reliable one his freedom.

Crate Soiling

Although dogs normally won't mess in their crates, some do. Occasional accidents shouldn't concern you, but if it happens every other day or more, try these suggestions:

- Remove all bedding in hopes he'll be repulsed by having nothing other than his body to absorb the mess.
- Use a smaller crate so he only has enough room to turn in place.
- Teach him to enter and exit his crate on command. ("Go to your bed/spot.")
- Place his food and water in the open crate to encourage a better association about being in there; then remove it when he's enclosed.

Maintaining a Schedule

Most puppies leave their litter to enter their new home at about two months of age. At this age, the pups eat a lot, drink a lot, and have limited ability to control their elimination and no comprehension that that might be important. Feeding and potty times should be adjusted to help puppy reach his potential in the housetraining department as quickly as possible. At two to four months of age most pups need to relieve themselves after waking up, eating, playing, sleeping, and drinking. At four months, the puppy may be developed like an adult internally, but expect him to behave like a puppy.

To housetrain effectively, you need to establish a schedule that works for your family and will help your puppy learn the rules quickly. You will be amazed at how quickly your puppy learns if you stick to a schedule that has fixed times for eating, sleeping and exercising.

Sample Schedule

6:30 A.M.	Take puppy out immediately when you wake up
6:45 A.M.	Feed puppy breakfast
7:00 A.M.	Take puppy back outside
7:15 A.M.	Play with puppy while getting ready for the day
7:45 A.M.	Take puppy outside
8:00 A.M.	Crate puppy when family leaves
Noon	Take puppy outside
12:15 P.M.	Feed puppy lunch
12:30 P.M.	Take puppy outside
12:45 P.M.	Play with puppy
1:00 P.M.	Crate puppy if leaving the home again
5:00 P.M.	Take puppy outside
5:30 P.M.	Feed puppy dinner
5:45 P.M.	Take puppy outside
6:00 P.M.	Play with puppy for remainder of evening, with trips outside every few hours

Just before bedtime: Take puppy outside. No more water after this for the rest of the night. Crate puppy for the night. (Very young puppies may have to be taken out once during the night.)

Diet and Feeding

Feed specific amounts of high-quality puppy food at specific times. Pups should be fed three times a day up to three or four months of age, and after that can be fed twice daily for the rest of their lives. If your schedule requires you to be gone for six or more hours at a time, feedings can be disproportionate. Consider feeding a larger portion when you will be home for a few hours and will therefore be able to give him the opportunity to relieve himself.

Look for signs that the food you've chosen agrees with your puppy. He should maintain the proper weight and muscle tone, have a healthy sheen to his coat, and have plenty of energy. Gas, loose stools, constipation, itchy skin, bald patches, or listlessness indicate a problem that may be diet-related. Investigate possible solutions by consulting with your veterinarian. When switching food, do so gradually over a period of at least five days. To maintain the firmness of his stools begin with a 20:80 ratio of new to familiar foods, and switch the ratios by 10 to 20 percent daily.

Water

Puppies should have access to fresh, clean water at all times except while crated and two hours before bed. Allow your puppy ample opportunity to drink at least five times a day (perhaps give water every time he goes out to ensure adequate hydration).

For pups who urinate frequently, try restricting access to water. But before doing so, tell your veterinarian about your plans to see if he or she wants to perform any diagnostic tests to rule out bladder or urinary tract problems. In severe cases where, despite a clean bill of health, the pup still continually urinates, offer water only before taking him out to relieve himself. With pups who just can't seem to hold it throughout the night, withhold water for three hours before going to bed.

The "Potty Spot" and How to Eliminate Immediately

Teach your puppy to eliminate on command. This lesson is handy both when he is too distracted and won't potty or when he's on a surface that he's inclined not to potty on—for example, a kennel run, wet grass, or where other puppies have been. Others will go potty only if they're in a particular area or taken for a walk. By teaching your puppy to eliminate on command, you can get him to go where you want, when you want, and simplify the housetraining process. Here's how to do it.

Leash your puppy and take him to the Potty Spot. When he begins the sniffing and circling ritual that immediately precedes elimination, start chanting a phrase like "Potty, hurry up." What you say is unimportant, but it should sound melodic and should always be the same phrase. Use the same words for defecation and urination. After a week begin the chant as soon as you enter the potty area. Always praise when he does what you want and give him an extra-special reward of playtime in the yard or a stroll around the block.

If you take your puppy to his Potty Spot and he doesn't eliminate right away, take him back inside for a few more minutes until you're certain he needs to. Don't take your puppy outside, ask him to do his business, and take him for a walk whether he does or not.

⊙ ABOUT FACE!

Teach him that going potty right away means getting a walk. If you dash back inside after puppy's gone potty, he'll learn that the only way to get a walk out of you is to hold it—and the only way for you to take him out is to go in the house. Remember, reward him for doing the correct thing: pottying in his spot when you ask him. Then and only then should he be rewarded.

Remember, patience is the key with housetraining. Your puppy is learning!

Dealing with Accidents

No matter how careful you are, occasionally inappropriate elimination happens. If your puppy has an accident do the following:

- Never correct the puppy after the fact. Do scold yourself by saying, "How could I have let that happen?"
- If you catch him in the act, startle him by saying, "Ach" loudly or picking him up in midstream and carrying him outside to stop him.
- Clean up messes immediately. Remove debris and blot up any moisture, then use a cleaning solution, and finally treat the soiled area with an odor neutralizer.

Until your puppy is perfectly potty-trained, remember:

1. Puppies who can hold it for long periods while they're in their crate or at night are not necessarily well on their way to being housebroken. Don't judge his capacity by his behavior while crated. Metabolism slows down with inactivity, so even a totally untrained puppy may not soil for up to twelve hours when he's crated.

2. Puppies enjoy playing, observing, and investigating, and often forget about going potty when they're left alone outdoors. Don't let your puppy out without supervision and assume that he did his business.

3. Puppies often indicate when they want to go outdoors and play, instead of when they need to potty. Don't rely on or encourage him to tell you he wants to go out. Many puppies will indicate frequently and always eliminate when taken to the potty area. This causes bladder and bowel capacity and control to be underdeveloped.

Common Housetraining Problems

Leashing your puppy during potty breaks will enable you to keep your puppy moving and sniffing within the appropriate area, and thus speed the process of elimination. If you sense your puppy is about to become distracted from his duty of looking for a potty spot, use a light, quick jerk on the leash as you slowly move about the area yourself. If you don't get results within five minutes, take puppy back inside and put him in his crate for another ten minutes or so. Eventually he'll have to go, and then you can reward him for going outside in the designated spot.

 ABOUT FACE!

Only give your puppy a few minutes to potty. If you give him twenty minutes, he is likely to demand thirty next time. After a couple minutes, put him back in his crate long enough to make him thankful for the next potty opportunity you give him. As stated earlier, have your puppy earn playtime by pottying first and playing afterward. Potty breaks will be much less time-consuming if your puppy learns to associate the initial act of walking outdoors with the act of going potty, not playing.

Many owners make the mistake of continually taking a puppy out before he really needs to go. Although they do so hoping he won't soil the house, they are actually preventing him from developing the capacity to hold it. Since housetraining is a matter of teaching the puppy to control his bladder and bowels until he has access to the outdoors, taking the puppy out too frequently slows the housetraining process. When you think he doesn't need to go out but he does, try umbilical-cording or crating him for a half-hour before taking a walk.

How Long Will It Take?
Plan on a year or more to complete the housetraining process. Although your puppy may be flawless for days, weeks, or months, under certain conditions any puppy can backslide. Seemingly benign events such as these can cause housetraining regression:

- Changes in diet
- Weather changes (too hot, cold, or wet, or noisy thunderstorms) can make outings unproductive potty times
- New environments (vacation homes, new house, or friend's house) may be treated as an extension of his potty area
- Some medications (like allergy medications) and certain conditions (like hormone changes associated with estrus) can cause more frequent elimination

Submissive Urination

If your puppy wets when he greets people or is disciplined, he isn't having a housetraining problem. Uncontrollable and unconscious leaking of urine is common in puppies and certain breeds. If your pup has been given a clean bill of health by a veterinarian so that you know his problem isn't health related, work on the problem by:

- Never yelling, striking, or showing anger toward him
- Making your entrances and greetings devoid of emotion
- Avoiding eye contact, talking, and touching during emotional states
- Withholding water if you're going out for a short period of time, and giving lots of water after you've been able to take him out to relieve himself

Try to avoid vigorous petting, impassioned tones of voice, and strong eye contact. Only interact with a superficial, brief pat, calm word, or fleeting glimpse when you are sure his bladder is empty.

When he consistently responds without tinkling, test his control after he's had water. Gradually try a warmer approach, but be ready to turn off the affection and issue a command if it pleases the pee out of him.

Paper Training—Is It an Option?

Owning a small puppy offers lots of advantages. One of these is that if you don't want to walk him outdoors, you can teach him to eliminate on papers indoors. To start, get full-sized newspapers and a sixteen-square-foot, wire-mesh exercise pen, available from puppy supply catalogs or by special order from a pet shop. Place the pen on an easy-to-clean floor and line the bottom with newspapers opened flat out. For one week, keep your puppy in the fully papered pen anytime you aren't supervising or exercising. Then, put a bed in the pen and gradually reduce the papered portion to one full-sized newspaper, overlapping five sheets to ensure proper absorption. Once he is pottying on the paper, open up the pen within a small room or hall. When he consistently soils on the paper, gradually give him access to the house, room by room.

Once trained, some paper-trained puppies only go on their papers; others prefer the outdoors but will use papers if necessary. You can paper-train a previously outdoor-trained puppy and vice versa, but you'll avoid extra work by deciding what you want up front.

CHAPTER 8

Attention: Obedience Training

Here, you will learn how to get your recruited puppy to obey your commands. While basic training will teach a puppy how to behave properly in general, obedience training will give you the ability to get your dog to do what you want, when you want it to. Not only that, but obedience training is the foundation to advanced tricks.

SIT AND SIT/STAY

There are a couple of ways to teach "Sit" effectively. You could alternate methods to see if your puppy is really learning the command or just the associated actions.

Method 1: Teach the "Sit" command by putting your puppy on your left side, holding his collar with your right hand and putting your left hand on his loin just in front of his hip bones and behind his rib cage. Command "Sit" as you pull upward on his collar and push downward on his loin. Talk, pet, and praise, but don't let the puppy move. When necessary, reposition him by pushing him back into the sit as you tighten up on the collar.

Method 2: With a small, yummy treat in your hand, like a sliver of hot dog or cheese, get your puppy's attention. When his nose is sniffing at the treat in your hand, without letting him eat it, keep your fingers close to his nose and raise your hand up and back. In order for his nose to follow your hand, your puppy will have to raise his head, which will naturally cause his hindquarters to go down into a sit. Say, "Sit" while you're moving your hand, and as soon as puppy is in the sit position, give him the treat and praise, saying, "Good sit!" Do this only two or three times, then take a break.

Vary the Environment

To proof the "Sit," ask your pup to sit on a strange-feeling surface—plastic bubble wrap, gravel, or a wire grate. Place him in the "Sit." If he refuses, then try a more normal surface like wet blacktop, slippery linoleum, or sand. Then ask him to sit on something really comfortable like a thick rug, plush carpeting, or a pillow. Practice several times a day on the most difficult surfaces first, then medium, and finally easy. Consider the command mastered when he willingly obeys the first "Sit" on the strangest surface.

Advancing to Sit/Stay

To start off, hold the leash taut over your puppy's head. Say "Stay" in a firm voice, then take one step back from him. While looking at your puppy, count silently to three, then and praise your puppy. Do this once more, and if your puppy stays for the whole count of three, give him a big hug and do something else for a while. If your puppy moves his head or wags his tail, that's acceptable, but you should correct scooting forward, rotating, and attempts to stand by pulling up on the leash and repeat "Stay" firmly.

If your puppy tries to lie down, tighten the leash enough to prevent him from lowering comfortably into the down position and give him praise as he realizes he doesn't have enough slack to lie down. Loosen the lead and prepare to repeat this sequence many times during the next week of training if your puppy is one who is inclined to recline.

You may be wondering why you should care about lying down on the sit/stay if you're not thinking of doing any competitive obedience. The answer is simple: you need your puppy to sit, not lie down, so you can look in his mouth, administer medication or ear ointment, or wipe dirt off his paws. Say what you mean and mean what you say to avoid confusion in all areas of training.

Sit/Stay from Farther Away

Once your puppy understands stay with you close in front of him, you can start increasing your distance from him while still expecting him to stay in a sit. To do this, ask him to "Stay," and take three or four steps back. Silently count to three, then release with "Okay" and praise your puppy. Increase both the amount of time you ask him to Sit/Stay and the distance you walk away from him until you can walk out to the end of the leash and he holds a Sit/Stay for seven or eight seconds. What a good puppy!

When he's solid with sitting and staying from a distance, introduce distractions like stepping side to side, bending down, pulling forward lightly on the leash, or dropping food or toys in front of your puppy. This teaches him that no matter what your preoccupation or what activities surround him, he stays put. While creating distractions, as long as your puppy remains in the Sit/Stay, tell him "Good stay."

Stop movement immediately by 1) sliding your free hand down almost to the snap of the leash as you step toward your puppy; 2) quickly maneuvering your puppy back into place without saying a word; 3) pulling upward on the leash; or 4) moving back to the end of the leash.

Enforce Sit/Stays while you 1) address a postcard, 2) read the headlines, 3) pop in a video, 4) empty the garbage, 5) download a computer file, 6) tie your shoes, 7) wrap a gift, 8) get stuck on hold, 9) weed a flowerbed. When you no longer need to allow spare time for corrections, your puppy has mastered the sit/stay.

Basic Guidelines for "Stays"

- Just before leaving your puppy, use a hand signal along with your "Stay" command. To signal, flash the palm of your free hand, fingers down toward his eyes.

- Use distractions—people, places, movement, food, toys—to test him and confirm he's learning.

- Be acutely attentive, and move in to correct the instant your puppy begins leaving the "Stay" position; otherwise, he'll wonder what the correction was for.

- Correct silently. If your puppy didn't listen the first time, repeating yourself will only cause further confusion or disobedience. Let your hands and leash alone amend his error.

- Adjust the strength of your correction to your puppy's size, level of training, why he moved and how excited or distracted he is.
- Leave instantly.
- Finish all "Stays" by walking to the puppy's right side, giving praise.

DOWN

Again, there are a few ways to teach your puppy to Down.

Method 1: While your pup is sitting, place your thumb and index finger behind his shoulder blades and on either side of the backbone. Say, "Down" as you push down on his back and shoulders. When he's on the floor, praise by scratching his tummy.

Method 2: With your puppy in the sit position and a tasty treat in your hand, hold the treat near his nose so he gets interested in it. Without letting him eat it but so that his nose follows your hand, start to slowly lower your hand toward the floor and toward you. The idea is to get his front end to come down toward your hand and then follow your hand out until he's lying down.

Many puppies stand up while they follow the lure with their nose. You can either keep a hand on his hindquarters to keep them down, or you can sneak the food lure under a chair so that he has to scooch on his tummy to follow it. As soon as he's down, feed the treat and say, "Good down!" If your puppy braces when you try Method 1, use your right hand to pull his head down to the ground as you push. Another option is to push with the fingers of the left hand as you use your right hand to lift the front paw that is bearing most of his weight. If you still simply can't get him down, discontinue work on the down and concentrate on perfecting the sit/stay around distractions; rare is the puppy who resists the down after becoming completely cooperative on the sit.

Once your puppy knows what down means, practice rapid-fire downs by commanding "Down," giving praise and repeating the sequence for one minute, three times per training session. Exceptional puppies may learn the verbal "Down" command in a week. With an average of twenty repetitions per day, most puppies will down 50 percent of the time after one month. But getting certain puppies into the "Down" can look like a scene from all-star wrestling. It's better to deal with these shenanigans in your house than at the veterinarian's office, where similar protests will be common if you haven't done this homework to abolish tantrums.

Testing Your Puppy on the Down

- Eliminate your body language by putting your hands in your pockets and evaluating yourself in front of a mirror. Your mouth is the only part of your anatomy that should move when commanding "Down."
- Whisper the "Down" command.
- Turn your back and look over your shoulder at your puppy to give the command.
- Stand in the shower (without running the water), sit in your car, or lie on a bed, stairs, or sofa, ask your puppy to Down, and see if your command still has authority.

Advancing to Down/Stay

The Down/Stay command is an excellent one for your puppy to know. Then you can tell your puppy to lie down and stay for grooming and examinations, during meals, or as guests arrive, or just to calm your puppy. Don't move on to this unless your puppy can do a leash-length Sit/Stay around distractions and can "Down" on command. To start, ask your puppy to "Down," then say "Stay" in a firm voice. While he's down, examine his ears, eyes, teeth, and paws. Use a pull on the leash or a two-finger push to correct movements like crawling, rolling, or ascension. Praise him frequently when he cooperates.

Although there is no need for the puppy to stare at you while he is in the down stay, you should correct grass munching, sniffing, or licking himself by saying, "Ach" in a startling way to get his attention back on you. Praise when he looks at you, and reinforce the "Stay."

🐾 HEEL

Like the skill and art of dancing, the benefits of heeling stretch well beyond the exercise itself. Dancing is a wonderful form of recreation on the dance floor, but the posture, alignment, controlled energy, balance, and poise practiced in dance movements sashay into everyday tasks.

The Heel command teaches the puppy to walk on your left side regardless of your pace or direction and to sit when you stop. Gone are the days of him pulling ahead or dragging behind, weaving from side to side or getting underfoot during walks.

Trust and respect develop as you and your canine partner master the art of heeling. This newly formed bond will help you channel the puppy's energy more efficiently no matter what the task, challenge, or obstacle.

 ABOUT FACE!

As the puppy learns to heel and you learn how to teach him to move precisely, a deeper learning takes place. To remain in position, the puppy's awareness, watchfulness, and willingness grow. Since you need to watch your puppy very intently during the process, you'll develop a sense of knowing what the puppy is going to do before he does it—otherwise known as "reading" your puppy.

Your goal is to teach your puppy to maintain heel position, on your left side, with his shoulder aligned with yours, and his body three inches from your leg. The position is the same whether you're moving forward, turning, or standing still. When you stop, your puppy should sit automatically.

Before you begin, practice sneakaways for at least one week, until your puppy is attentive to you despite distractions. To begin, hold the leash in your right hand with your right thumb through the loop and four fingers holding the slack. Say, "[puppy's name], heel" as you begin walking. Prepare to stop by grabbing the collar with your right hand and using your left to place his rear end into a sitting position so his right front foot is alongside your left ankle.

As you walk along preparing to halt, control your puppy's position using the fold-over maneuver. Grab the leash with your left hand and hold it taut over puppy's head, then use your right to grip the braiding or stitching of the leash just above the snap. Next, take your left hand off the leash and use it to place puppy in a sit in perfect heel position as you halt.

If your puppy forges ahead, do a leash-length sneakaway. Drop the slack of the leash, grip the handle, hold your hands at your waistline, and run away. As the puppy returns to your side, return to the original leash grip, holding the slack, as you continue walking. If your puppy lags behind, say, "Good puppy!" as you spring ahead by taking a puddle jump with your left leg first. As you do this, your left thigh will pull the leash, and your puppy, back to the heel position. The jump ahead will also prevent the puppy from crossing behind you to the right side.

Going from Heel to Sit

Before you begin this, your puppy should reliably sit 80 percent of the time when you ask him. He shouldn't need to be touched or retold. What you want him to do is stop heeling and go into the sit position. Here's what to do.

1. Command, "[puppy's name], heel" and move off on your left foot.
2. Prepare to stop by gathering the leash in both hands.
3. As you finish your last step, pull up on the leash, and say, "Sit."

You'll need to practice this over and over. Don't wear yourself or your puppy out. If he doesn't get it the first time, try once more and, if you're successful, end on a positive note. If he doesn't get it the second time, go on to something else and start again later.

Learning to Heel with Turns

You'll need to practice turning while you're heeling. This helps stop tendencies to heel too far from or too close to you, and to correct slight forging and sniffing of the ground. You want to practice turning sharply.

Use the "Jackie Gleason left turn" to stop slight forging, crowding, and sniffing of the ground: Turn ninety degrees to the left, then step perpendicularly into your puppy so your left foot and leg slide or step behind his front legs. Shuffle into him until he becomes attentive and moves back to the left side. Practice slowing your pace abruptly, then turn left immediately if your puppy's shoulder is even one inch ahead of yours. If your puppy attempts to cross in front of you to the right side, tighten the leash with your left hand as you continue to step into him.

To stop wideness, sniffing, or lagging, use puddle jump following a right turn. Pivot ninety degrees to your right on your left foot, take a large step in your new direction with the right foot and leap forward with your left leg as if you were jumping over a puddle. As you jump the puddle you should feel the leash against your left thigh, pulling the puppy forward. Steady your leash by holding your right hand against your right hip as you leap.

Jump and praise simultaneously to motivate your puppy. Hold the leash in your right hand so the slack will remain in front of your thighs as you jump.

COME

One of the most frustrating things for dog owners is a dog that won't come when called. So that you don't become one of those owners, you want your puppy to learn that when he comes to you when you call him, he will be made to feel like the world's best dog. Coming to you should always be a positive experience. Reward your pup with exuberant praise, tasty treats, a game of fetch, more time on your walk, whatever it takes to let him know that he did the right thing.

Your puppy will learn this if you make it easy for him to succeed by starting with short "comes" and progressing to distance "comes." Your sneakaway training should have taught him that he gets the most praise when he comes to you.

Reeling in Your Puppy

Leash your puppy and take him for a walk. If he begins sniffing something, gazing around, or meandering off, call "Buddy, come!" Immediately back up quickly as you reel the leash, praising enthusiastically. Kneel down when puppy arrives, heaping him with verbal praise and occasionally slipping him a super-tasty treat.

Some puppies will come toward you but stay out of reach or dart right past you. Some owners, without realizing it, encourage the puppy to cut his approach and stay further away by attempting to cradle, caress, or hug the puppy. Petting the puppy as he arrives can create or worsen these recall problems because extending your arms makes it appear you are protecting the space in front of you. Instead, use verbal praise to acknowledge, encourage, and congratulate the puppy's arrival and keep your hands to yourself until he's right with you.

⭐ ABOUT FACE!

If a puppy does not come when she is called, it's annoying for sure, but even more importantly, it's dangerous. Make sure your puppy knows to come to you when she is called, and not when she feels like it, to avoid situations like speeding cars and unsuspecting people.

After practicing your reeling recalls twenty or so times, your puppy is probably running toward you faster than you can reel. Now see if he'll leave distractions when you stand still and call, "Come." If he doesn't respond promptly, use a sharp, fast, horizontal jerk toward you as you praise and back up. If he does respond to your command, praise and continue to back up, praising as he nears you.

The goal you want to reach next is to teach your puppy to stop and come when called even if he's running away or you're following him. That sounds like asking a lot of him, doesn't it? But remember again, if you practice asking him to come several times a day and you make it rewarding for him every time he does so, why wouldn't he want to be attentive to you?

Here's what to do: Three times this week create a situation that will cause your puppy to forget his training and pull toward a distraction. For example, ask a fellow puppy owner to go with you on a walk. Instruct him to walk his puppy about ten feet ahead of you. Your puppy is likely to want to catch up to them. As you are walking directly behind your puppy, ask him to come. If he responds, what a good boy! Praise and crouch down to reward him. If he doesn't respond, tug on his leash, back up, call him again, and praise when he turns toward you. Then reel him in.

If your puppy stops when you call him but he doesn't come to you, stay put. Don't chase after him. Pull the leash to let him know you want him to come toward you, then ask again. He should do what you want.

If you intend to call your puppy from a distance, first attach a long, lightweight line to your puppy's collar. When he's distracted, position yourself over the line and call him. Praise him the entire time he's coming toward you, from the time he begins taking his first step toward you until you release him. If the puppy ignores your request, correct him by grabbing the line and using "wrap, run, and praise"—wrap the line around your hand twice just above where your thumb attaches to your hand, make a fist around the line, and anchor your hand on your waist as you run away from your puppy. When the line starts to pull him, he will have to follow you. Praise all the way that it takes for him to reach you.

Reliability on the Recall

The goal of this is that whether his last recall was a minute ago or a week ago, he will reliably obey the come command. Before you begin, perfect sneakaways around distractions and practice your recalls with distractions as described previously.

Twice weekly, for thirty minutes, take your puppy to a new location, one he will eagerly explore and continually investigate. Try parks, fields, a friend's yard, or anywhere you know he'll want to investigate. Attach a very long 50- to 200-foot light line to his collar and allow him to roam. Put on your gloves and every five minutes or so, when he least expects it and is running away, call and "wrap, run, and praise."

Basic Guidelines for "Come"

- Don't put your authority at risk by calling come when your puppy may not obey and you know you can't enforce.
- Standardize your voice, always using the same enthusiastic tone that suggests urgency, to say, "Buddy, come!"
- Appeal to your puppy's chase instinct and help ensure a faster recall by moving away after calling come.
- Praise enthusiastically while he approaches. If you wait until he arrives, your lack of commitment will reduce his commitment to the process, too.
- Squat to acknowledge his final approach and arrival.
- Make him come all the way to you. If you suspect your puppy isn't going to make a direct approach, move opposite from the puppy's line of movement so he gets pulled toward you.
- Periodically delay the release as your puppy's recall becomes faster and more reliable.

🐾 WAIT

A request that comes in very handy around the house is "Wait." Use this to ask your puppy to wait at the door, go in or out of the door, or when you're out of sight.

The "Stay" command means freeze in the sit, down, or stand position and, therefore, is very restrictive. The "Wait" command, though, allows your puppy to move about, but only within certain areas. You can use it to keep your puppy in the car or out of the kitchen. The only thing "Wait" has in common with "Stay" is that both last until the next direction is given, twenty seconds or twenty minutes later.

Teach the "Wait" command at doorways first. Choose a light-weight door and estimate how wide your puppy's front end is. Open the door two inches more than that as you command "Wait." Stand there with your hand on the knob of the partially open door, ready to bump the puppy's nose with it should he attempt to pass through the opening. Be sure never to shut the door while correcting. Instead, leave the door open with your hand on the door handle, ready to stop attempted departures with an abrupt and silent bump of the door. If necessary, butt him with a quick movement that makes it appear the door is snapping at him every time he tries to peer or charge out. Leash your puppy so if your attempts to deter him fail and he successfully skips across the border, you can step on the leash and prevent his escape.

Practice at familiar and unfamiliar doors as a helper tries to coerce your puppy to leave. Your helper can talk to the puppy and drop food, but your helper shouldn't call your puppy. As your helper remains on the opposite side of the door, engage in lively conversation to teach your puppy that even when you are preoccupied, the "Wait" command is enforced. When that lesson has been learned you'll no longer need the leash.

CHAPTER 9

R+R with Other Soldiers

When the socialization of recruits is neglected, they never reach their potential as good little soldiers. They're less adaptable, harder to live with, and, in many observations, less happy. A dog that's received frequent and early socialization thrives on environment changes, interactions, and training procedures.

Start Socializing!

People often assumed that fearful dogs have been mistreated by a prior owner or some other person who has had contact with the dog. More commonly, however, dogs are fearful or phobic because they lack early experience with different types of people, sounds, and experiences, including other dogs. Genetics can also play a fairly large role in shaping a dog's fearful behavior, and some breeds have shyness as a common, though undesirable, trait.

Breeding

A good breeder is committed to turning out puppies that are healthy, well adjusted, and ready for life. They screen their potential puppy buyers and make sure they educate each person who buys a puppy so that they train and socialize their puppies appropriately. The reality is you get what you pay for, and quality puppies from good breeders don't come cheap.

If you feel your dog's problems stem from a genetic component, it is still possible to train her. Even in well-bred dogs with conscientious breeders, some puppies can be more fearful than their littermates. If the shyness is identified early enough, and intensive socialization and training is implemented, a lot of progress can be made in a relatively short period of time. The earlier the problem is identified, the better the prognosis. Certain breeds can be more prone to fearfulness, but any dog can grow up being fearful and suspicious of new people and experiences.

A genetic predisposition to noise sensitivity is common in many breeds used for hunting and sporting purposes. Dog breeders who truly care will breed out these traits by choosing only the friendliest, most confident dogs for their breeding programs. If you are looking for a puppy of a breed that has fearful tendencies, ask lots of questions about the parents' temperaments, meet both parents before purchasing the pup, and choose a breeder who has someone perform the puppy aptitude test on all of their litters. Dogs that are carefully bred by knowledgeable, caring people should be friendly and outgoing regardless of their breed.

Social Development
If you feel your dog's fearfulness is a result of a lack of early socialization, and your dog is still under a year, get out there and

get busy. The earlier you start to change this, the more successful your training program will be. The longer you wait, the harder it will be to change.

Consider enrolling your dog in a well-organized group training class. Be honest with your instructor about what your goals are, and ask if a group class would be an appropriate place to start with your dog. Consider a doggie day care facility; there are often ones that take on special cases where the staff is knowledgeable about these problems. They can help make sure your dog has an enjoyable day. Don't be afraid to ask questions, and be flexible and consistent with your end of the commitment.

ABOUT FACE!

Try to be patient with your recruit during this training process. If you lose your patience and yell, this undoes all the work you just did and makes your pup even more fearful than she was before, because she now associates training with yelling. To make your pup more socially motivated and confident, you need to put confidence in her!

Getting a puppy from a person who has been raising dogs for many years and knows how to provide the right kind of environment will save you years of time in the long run. If a puppy misses out on these critical early social periods and is not raised in an environment that stimulates him to explore and learn about his world, he will be a fearful, phobic adult dog. Shyness, fears, and fear-related aggression is most likely the result of a lack of socialization than past abuse or mistreatment. Often abuse is used as the excuse for dogs that are fearful or aggressive when in reality it is a lack of early socialization that is the problem. However, there are dogs out there that have been mistreated and are fearful and skittish as a result of learning that strange people and places are scary and dangerous. The same advice applies if your dog has been mistreated; sit down and develop a plan, and then get out there and train your dog!

Confidence

Fearful dogs don't have to stay that way forever. In fact, they should not be fearful at all, as that hinders the socialization process. Fearful dogs are very likely to lash out when suddenly put into a situation that they do not understand or are not familiar with. Confidence is the key to good social skills! With lots of patience and careful training, you can help your dog enjoy life just a little more. Keep in mind, however, that building confidence in a fearful dog is time consuming; don't expect miracles overnight. Be flexible in your plans. Be sure to make room for regression, and have a plan as to how you will handle it. Being prepared for setbacks will also help your dog gain confidence more quickly, since her handler will simply shift plans and continue on rather than panic, flounder, and confuse her.

Review the section on targeting, and once you've got your dog easily following your hand, transfer the target to another person. Find a helper that the dog knows and have her offer her hand as a target for your dog to touch. You may have to go back to the early steps and have the helper start off with a treat in her hand at first.

Gradually increase the distance so that your dog will go across the room to touch the person's outstretched hand. Verbally label the behavior Go Say Hello. Congratulations! You now have a new game to play with your dog and a way to increase his confidence around new people. Practice at every opportunity and be sure to have a backup plan in case he is too fearful to go and target. Having a plan will make it so that you will transition smoothly and your dog will barely notice that you've changed plans.

Another technique for building your pup's confidence involves playing an unpleasant trigger noise at a very low volume or keeping a scary person or thing at enough distance so that the dog notices it but does not react fearfully to it. A good rule of thumb is that if the dog won't take a treat or play with you, the volume is too high or the distance is too close. Increase the volume gradually, or bring the person or thing closer, so that eventually the dog will ignore it all together and continue to take treats and play.

This process, called systematic desensitization, involves interacting with the dog in a positive way, be it with a game of fetch or teaching tricks, so as to help the dog develop a more positive association with the feared noise. The dog starts to associate the feeling of being relaxed around the scary noise or object and eventually the volume can be increased and the distance decreased until the dog will accept the new thing as part of his environment and no longer finds it threatening.

Another technique some dog owners use is to play recordings of the outside world before socialization—rainstorms, other dogs barking, children laughing and playing—so the dog will be familiar with these sounds. This helps prevent your dog from being fearful or lashing out at unfamiliar noises and sounds.

Teaching tricks would be a great way for the dog to associate fun with noise. If you move slowly enough you will find that having fun learning and performing tricks is incompatible with acting fearful. With enough patience and practice, you will have a dog that is able to get over his fears and become a social little puppy.

Rules to Follow

No matter what your house rules are, the most important thing is that you have them. A dog that knows what is expected of her will know that someone else is going to take care of her. This alone will give her more confidence. House rules can be flexible, but not until your dog is more confident. The more strict and consistent the rules are, the quicker the dog will be to trust that you can take care of her and the more she will look to you for leadership.

There are several things you can do to help raise your dog's confidence level and make it more likely that your training program will be successful.

- **Avoid reinforcing fearful behavior.** Petting and talking soothingly to the dog or picking him up reinforces fearful behavior. A hands-off approach where you state that everything is fine will send the message to your dog that there is nothing to fear.
- **No punishment—ever!** There is never a reason for punishment in a situation where a dog is fearful. If a dog is frightened,

she is in an emotional state, not a learning state. Physical or verbal correction will only convince her that there really is something to fear. Punishment may even bring out aggression if your dog feels threatened and vulnerable. Avoid any type of correction; it won't get you where you want to go.

- **Safety first.** Keep the leash on at all times in public and make the exits in your house escape-proof. Deny your dog access to the front door, for instance, if she is constantly looking to dash out or tends to panic during thunderstorms or with loud noises.
- **Exercise and mental stimulation.** Dogs that lack confidence need exercise more than ever. Chasing a ball, hide-and-seek, learning tricks, agility, fly ball, or any of the various dog sports are all excellent ways for your dog to release her energy reserves and the tensions of the day.

These rules are guides to improve and boost your dog's confidence, so when she is ready to become social—she'll be the belle of the ball!

Turn Your Pup into a Social Butterfly!

Usually, beginning the socialization process consists of providing a safe environment for your dog to explore. Concentrate on four areas: socializing your dog to people, places, things, and other animals. In unpredictable or potentially unsafe situations, keep your dog leashed. That lets you prevent a wobbly youngster from trying to pick him up, and you can keep him off the sidewalk as a skateboard zips by.

Socialize him to people, making sure he gets plenty of experiences with both genders and a variety of races and ages. Go to the park, a parade, the beach, outside a shopping center, or to an airport if you're bold enough to pretend you belong there. Occasionally, leave your puppy in the care of a trustworthy, level-headed friend for a minute, an hour, or a day. Treat the situation as a nonevent so your puppy is less likely to experience separation anxiety.

 ABOUT FACE!

Think about items people carry and equipment they use. Expose your dog to wheelchairs, canes, bicycles, lawn mowers, Big Wheels, and roller skates.

Take your puppy as many places as possible so he becomes a savvy traveler who is accustomed to elevators, stairways, manholes, and grates. Acclimate him to walking on a variety of surfaces such as gravel, wire, sand, cobblestone, linoleum, and brick. Because some dogs prefer to eliminate only in their own backyard, teach him to eliminate on command in different areas, so weekend trips and the like won't be a problem. If you want to foster enjoyment of the water and your dog isn't a natural pond puppy, walk him on-leash on the shoreline. Once he is at ease with that, venture into the water. Gently tighten the leash as you go, forcing him to swim a couple of feet before you let him return to the shoreline. Never throw any dog into the water.

Let him get to know other animals—dogs, cats, chickens, horses, goats, birds, guinea pigs, and lizards. Often, upon meeting a new species, a puppy is startled, then curious, and finally some become bold or aggressive. For his own protection and for the protection of the other animal, always keep him leashed so you can control his distance and stop unwanted behaviors by enforcing obedience commands.

If you want to socialize your dog because you have more than one dog, or would just like him to be social with dogs he meets, start by letting him play with other pups. Keep this in mind, however: rough play among dogs is usually harmless amusement for humans and canines. If they're generally friendly and tolerant of one another, dogs or puppies rarely inflict injury. They will get noisy and animated: growling, barking, squealing, tumbling, and dragging one another by convenient body parts (such as ears and limbs) is common. Break up the game only if one of the dogs is being endangered, or if the play occurs in a formal living room or while people desire quiet. Don't raise your voice to break them up. Instead, leash one or both dogs and give a subdued command to stop, accompanied by a jerk of sufficient strength to ensure that they follow your request. An important tip to remember when introducing a new puppy to your current dog or cat, or bringing another animal into your new puppy's home, is that the established pet in the house considers your home its territory.

Whatever you are socializing your puppy to—animals, objects, or people—approach in a relaxed manner and avoid any situation that would intimidate the average puppy, such as a group of grade schoolers rushing at him. Be prepared for three reactions: walking up to check it out and sniff, apprehensive barking with hackles raised, or running away. No matter his response, remain silent. In the first, and by the way, best, scenario, he is thinking rationally and investigating his environment. Don't draw attention to yourself by talking, praising, or petting. Allow him to explore uninterrupted. This good boy is entertaining himself and being educated at the same time. If your puppy lacks confidence or displays fear, don't console him, because this will reinforce his fear. Use the leash to prevent him from running away. If he is still slightly uncomfortable, drop some tasty bits of food (such as slivers of hot dogs) on the ground. Most puppies will relax after a nibble or two because the uncomfortable situation has been positively associated with food.

 ABOUT FACE!

Dogs are very territorial and fiercely protective of their home, family and belongings. If possible, always try to introduce pets to each other in neutral territory, maybe in a friend's yard or in a park. It's very important to make sure neither of the animals feels threatened or becomes a bully.

If loud noises frighten your puppy, desensitize him by allowing him to create racket. Offer him a big metal spoon with a little peanut butter on it. Give him an empty ½ gallon or gallon milk jug with the cap removed and a bit of squeeze cheese in the rim to bat around. It won't be long before he is creating hubbub and loving it. Of course, if the clamoring drives you nuts, feel free to limit his playtime with these items. Also socialize your puppy to walking on leash, riding in the car, and being examined and groomed.

Riding in the Car

As soon as your puppy is large enough, teach him to enter and exit the car on command. Practice this by leashing him, walking him up to the car, and commanding him to go in as you give him a boost. Invite him out of the car by calling "come" as you gently pull the leash. Practice several of these, several times a day, until he goes in and out on command. Even before your puppy is ready for that lesson, decide where you'd like him to ride. Crating is the safest option. If it isn't the most convenient, try a doggy seatbelt, which is available at many pet shops or by mail order. Don't feed your puppy for hours prior to riding if he has any tendency toward carsickness. It is also a good idea to keep the air temperature inside the car comfortably cool (if you roll down a window, choose one that your puppy cannot stick his head out of). Additionally, you'll reduce the chance of motion sickness by avoiding bumpy roads and abrupt stops or turns.

Going to the Infirmary and Groomer

It is extremely important to train your dog to accept grooming and examinations, especially for his health and well-being. As to the specific grooming procedures, techniques, and products to use, talk to an expert such as a breeder, handler, or groomer.

Begin by acclimating your pup to handling of all areas of his head. Look in his eyes, ears, and mouth, and check out his feet (feel the toes, pads, and nails) and body (run your hands along his legs, underbelly, chest, and tail). Touch his gumline, his teeth (don't forget the molars), and inside his ears. Hold his collar with one hand so you can jerk it to settle a feisty pup. Open his mouth as you would do if you were giving a pill—gently grasp the upper jaw with one hand and the lower jaw with the other, fingers behind the canine (fang) teeth. Try all these things when he is standing on the floor and also when he is on a table or other small elevated surface such as the top of a washing machine. If possible, tie a leash to an overhead pipe or ceiling hook so that the snap hangs down just low enough to attach it to his collar to create a noose-like arrangement. And just like a professional groomer, never leave your dog unattended when noosed.

Additionally, teach your puppy to accept being rolled on his side and examined or groomed. Start by practicing the "settle position." Kneel on the ground at his side and reach around him as if you were giving a bear hug. Clasp his legs on the opposite side and gently roll him by moving his legs under his body and toward you. Then, with your hand holding the rear leg, slide his bottom between your knees and straddle him. Place your hands, palms down, on his chest with your thumbs facing one another below his armpits to prevent him from wriggling away. Remain still and calm. When he relaxes, release him by saying "Okay" as you loosen your hold. Practice this procedure on seven- to eighteen-week-old pups.

The Last Word on Socialization

Perhaps your veterinarian advised you against exposing your dog while his immune system is developing, but you fear the risks of neglecting his socialization during this critical period. Though you may not be able to walk him around the big city, you can start a socialization program in your own barracks with some more helpful tips:

- Desensitize him to noises by letting him play with an empty plastic half-gallon or gallon milk jug or big metal spoon. Also, remember the tape recorder technique that involves playing outside world sounds!
- Accustom him to walking on a variety of surfaces such as bubble wrap, big plastic bags, or chicken wire. Put a treat in the middle so he gets rewarded for his bravery.
- If his experiences with meeting new people are limited, you can get creative with costumes. Wear hats, masks, and capes, and walk with a cane, or a limp, skip, and hop.
- Handle him as described in the grooming and examination section.
- Take him for car rides with permission from your veterinarian.

CHAPTER 10

Special Forces and Color Guard: Some Fun Tricks!

I t can't be work all the time at canine boot camp; your new recruit needs to learn to have some fun, too! Here are some tricks that can make your soldier shine!

🐾 KINDERGARTEN TRICKS

Teaching tricks does not need to be a complicated task. Even novice trainers can teach a dog an entertaining trick, giving both trainer and dog a sense of accomplishment. The tricks that follow are simple and easy to teach, and are even appropriate for puppies, with their limited understanding of the training game.

Teaching Simple Tricks

Each dog has a unique style of learning, and it is your job as her trainer to find the best techniques to explain to her whatever trick you are trying to teach. The amount of sessions to learn one trick will vary according to the dog, so just know that as long as you are progressing from one step to the next, you are succeeding.

Keep in mind as you work on new tricks with your dog:

- Only introduce one new skill per session. Skipping around too much will confuse the dog and might discourage sensitive dogs altogether.
- Remember that the shaping outlines are building blocks toward an end goal. As with most goals, teaching a trick is accomplished by starting at the beginning with the first step and progressing through to the end by adding each step, one at a time, until all the steps come together to form a trick.
- Once you've established a few basics, it's a good idea to review previous skills or steps as a warm-up.
- Try to work in two or three sessions per day to see real improvement and accomplishment in a week's time, but there should be at least two hours between sessions. Dogs take time to process what they have learned and sometimes a rest gives them time to put more challenging concepts together.

Polite Pawing

Many dogs can do these simple tricks with very little prompting because they already use their paws to play with toys or get your attention. If your dog falls into that category, teaching these tricks should be fairly straightforward.

Give Your Paw

Give Your Paw may be the most natural trick for dogs prone to pawing. However, it also serves as the foundation for other paw-oriented tricks, so master this one first. The shaping steps for teaching Give Your Paw are:

1. Find out what usually gets your dog to paw at you and use it to get him to do it. As your dog's paw is in the air, click and treat.

2. Repeat this fifteen to twenty times until your dog is offering his paw readily.

3. Now, leave your hand outstretched and wait your dog out; don't prompt him in any other way and see what happens. If he lifts his paw at all, click and treat.

4. If after a few seconds he does not lift his paw, go back to helping him for another ten to fifteen repetitions before you try again. You want the dog to understand that lifting his paw is what gets the click and treat to happen.

5. If you are using your outstretched hand as the prompt that gets your dog to give his paw, this can be turned into the cue for the behavior. Show your hand and click and treat your dog as he is stretching out his paw.

6. Add the verbal cue Give Your Paw when your dog is raising his paw to slap your hand on a regular basis.

7. Practice in different environments with various distractions, being careful not to overwhelm your dog. If the behavior falls apart in the new place don't be afraid to make things easier for him and help him out.

High Five

The High Five is just a variation of the Give Your Paw trick with a few minor adjustments.

1. Teach your dog to target your hand with her paw for a click and treat.
2. Present your hand as the target in various positions until you can hold your hand up, palm facing the dog with fingers toward the ceiling. Click and treat your dog for touching your hand with her paw.
3. Practice this until your dog is quickly raising her paw when she sees you put your hand up.
4. Verbally label the behavior High Five when it is happening on a regular basis.
5. Add in distractions and work on having her do it with other people as well.

Calm Canines

Training involves many elements, but there are two things to remember. First, make the most of your dog's natural behavior, as the paw tricks demonstrate. Secondly, use training to elicit desired behavior, such as behaving in the presence of other people or dogs. The following tricks will help your dog remain calm, and will put your guests at ease, too.

Bow

Teaching your dog to Bow on command will not only make for a flashy trick but also may help you put a visiting dog at ease. Dogs invite each other to play in this position and it can be an excellent way for your dog to learn to make friends. To perform this trick, the dog starts from a standing position and lowers the front half of its body until its elbows touch the floor.

1. Starting your dog in a standing position, hold your hand below her chin (about 3 inches) and get her to touch your hand, then click and treat.
2. Gradually make it harder by placing your hand closer to the ground in increments of several inches each time. Click and treat your dog for making an attempt to lower her head further to touch your hand.
3. When your hand is resting on the ground, click and treat your dog for touching it with her nose without lying all the way down. If your dog continually lies down, raise your hand by several inches for a while before continuing on.
4. Make sure you watch your dog carefully and click and treat any effort she makes to bend her elbows.
5. Once your dog will lower her top half, start giving her less help by removing your target hand before she touches it.
6. Fade the hand target until she drops her head when you just begin to make the motion with your hand.
7. Increase the difficulty by only clicking and treating those repetitions where she lowers her head fast.

8. Increase the difficulty by increasing the duration (length of time the dog holds the behavior) by adding a Hold It or Stay command. To increase the duration of the behavior, delay the click by one or two seconds and gradually increase the time.

9. Add a verbal cue like Bow just before she performs the behavior. Take it on the road and perform in new places.

Play Dead

Teaching your dog to Play Dead is a show-stopping trick that is sure to make even non-dog lovers sit up and take notice. This trick requires the dog to lay on his back with his paws in the air and hold it until released.

1. Get your dog to lie down, then click and treat.

2. Use a treat to roll your dog onto his side; click and treat.

3. Fade the lure by doing six repetitions in a row and then trying the seventh repetition without the lure, clicking and treating the dog for performing the behavior.

4. Reintroduce the lure to get him to roll onto his back, then click and treat. Fade the lure after the sixth repetition.

5. Go back and put all three steps together so that he performs them all in one continuous motion for one click and treat.

6. Fade the lure by working with food for six repetitions then without food for two repetitions. Go back and forth until your dog responds the same with or without food. Note:

The way you hold your hand will become the exaggerated cue that starts the behavior.

7. Change the old cue to a new cue by offering the new cue before the motion you used to get the behavior started. Pointing your thumb and forefinger like a gun and saying "bang!" is very flashy, however if you are uncomfortable with guns or are showing this trick to someone who is, feel free to mix it up with cues.

8. Work on speed by only rewarding the dog for quick responses to the new signal. Decide on how many seconds he has to start the behavior and click and treat even before he finishes. Clicking in the middle of the behavior is what builds speed.

Who Loves an Audience?

Although some of your training is behavior modification, some of it is just plain fun. Once you've trained a well-behaved, socially acceptable dog, let everyone in on the games!

Roll Over

Roll Over requires your dog to lie down flat on his stomach, roll all the way over, and get back on his feet. Though the concept is simple, this is not always an easy trick for your dog to perform. Long-back breeds like dachshunds or basset hounds may not be as good at this trick as other breeds due to the way they are built.

Pay close attention to your dog to be sure he's not hurting or twisting his back. If, despite your best efforts, your dog refuses to get on his back, skip this trick and try another. Your dog may be sore or uncomfortable and this may be his only way to express it. If possible, teach this trick on a soft surface like a towel or carpet so the dog is more comfortable.

1. Get your dog to lie down with his belly touching the ground, and click and treat.
2. Use a treat or a toy to turn your dog's head until he flops over on one hip, and click and treat.
3. Use a treat or toy held close to your dog's shoulder to get him completely on his side, and click and treat.
4. Gradually move the treat or toy while he's chewing on it, to move him onto his back and then eventually all the way over. This step often takes many attempts before the dog is comfortable enough to be on his back.
5. Click and treat small efforts to move toward the treat at first before you get him to move further to get his click and treat. If you make it too hard to earn a click your dog will quit on you and think it's no fun.
6. When your dog is rolling, it's time to start fading out all the extra cues and make him offer more before you click.
7. Once he can roll over with just this little bit of help you can begin to verbally label this trick Roll Over. Whatever you are doing with your hand or fist could be a hand signal for the behavior as well.
8. Add in distractions one at a time and be prepared to help him complete the trick if he has trouble concentrating.

Spin

Spinning involves your dog turning in a complete circle in either direction. As your dog gets good at this, you can have her keep spinning until you tell her to stop. If you've tried to teach this trick using a lure or food treat, you probably realized how difficult it is to get rid of the lure. Instead, use targeting either with your hand or with a target stick to show your dog what you want her to do.

1. Use your hand as a target and with your dog facing you, get her to follow your hand a quarter of the way around, then click and treat.

2. Now, leave your target hand at the quarter-way mark and wait until your dog touches it with her nose on her own before you click and treat. Practice this until she's offering it readily.

3. Next, just before she touches your hand, move your target hand to the halfway point and click and treat your dog for following it, but before she actually touches it.

4. At this point, as you drop your hand she may spin the rest of the way around, but continue to click and treat for the halfway point in order to build speed.

5. Use your target hand to start the dog turning, but then pull it away quickly. Click and treat your dog for attempting to turn without the target to guide her.

6. Time the click so that you're clicking the dog for being at the halfway point.

7. Continue to minimize your target hand and click the dog for continuing to turn without your help.

8. Fade the target hand to just a motion to the left or right.

9. Fade the target to a simple left or right cue. A pointed index finger would be appropriate as a final signal.

Once you and your dog have mastered ten in a row, you can begin working on speed. Set a time limit in which your dog must perform the behavior, and click and treat only those repetitions that meet the goal. To train your dog to spin in the other direction, simply go back to the first step and work your way through.

 SOCIAL GRACES

Your dog will shake hands and bow—that's something! Well, you can certainly expand his social skills to include a few kisses and pleasant conversation. The joy of having a dog is your interaction with each other. These next two behaviors make the most of that.

Kiss Me

Teaching this behavior utilizes a combination of free shaping and luring. You are catching the dog in the act of doing the behavior and rewarding it, but you are getting the behavior started by prompting it first. The shaping steps for teaching Kiss Me are:

1. Using food to initially excite your dog is the key. Feed him a few small pieces of a treat and eat a few yourself, then stick your chin out and wait.

2. At the first sign of any attempt to lick you, click and treat.

3. Try putting the treats in your mouth and showing him they're there. Click and treat any attempt to lick you.

4. Add the verbal cue Kiss right before he's going to offer the behavior. Click and treat as the behavior happens.

5. Fade the food by showing it to the dog and putting it away on a counter or table and commanding Kiss. When he kisses, click and treat and run and get the treat.

6. Repeat this until the dog is beginning to offer the kiss as soon as you stick out your chin.

Speak

Luring and free shaping, or a combination of the two, are the best tools for teaching this trick. The trick itself requires your dog to bark on cue.

1. Find something that causes your dog to bark, like a knock on the door or holding a treat out of range. Click and treat her when she barks.

2. Repeat at least twenty to twenty-five times.

3. Fake the antecedent to barking (the knock), and if your dog starts to bark, click and treat.

4. Verbally label the behavior Speak just before your dog barks.

5. Don't click and treat for any barking other than the one you ask for.

6. If she barks at inappropriate times, be obvious about turning your upper body away to let her know that extraneous barking will not be rewarded.

These simple tricks are the best opportunity for you and your dog to build a trusting and cooperative relationship. You'll develop a better understanding of how your dog thinks, and what motivates her, and your dog will learn to read your cues. Take the time to train your dog well—you'll both get the best results that way.

🐾 RETRIEVING TRICKS

Any dog can learn to pick something up in its mouth and bring it to his handler. Although some dogs have an instinctive talent to perform this behavior, even the most reluctant dog can learn using operant conditioning by means of a clicker and treats.

Using a novel object will make it more likely that your dog will at least investigate it, giving you a starting point for shaping the retrieve. Teach the retrieve by breaking it down into the most basic steps so that it will be resistant to falling apart later. The shaping steps to teach the retrieve are as follows:

1. Put an item on the floor three feet away from your dog.
2. Click and treat him for moving toward it.
3. Click and treat him for touching the object with his nose.
4. Repeat this step a dozen times and then withhold the click.
5. If he mouths the object at all, click and treat.

6. Once your dog is mouthing the object, withhold the click until he picks up the object.

7. Delay the click once more and build the time he will hold the object.

8. Add distance by putting the object a short distance away at first and gradually increasing it.

9. Label the retrieve Take It as the dog is picking up the object.

10. Label the release of the object Give or Leave It.

Get the Mail/Newspaper

This trick works well if you have a door slot for your mail or you have a daily newspaper that gets delivered to your door. For this trick, your dog has to go to where the mail or paper is kept, pick up the item, bring it to you, and release it into your hand.

1. Teach your dog to carry nonessential letters and junk mail without stopping to shred them before you use the real thing. ("The dog ate the mortgage bill" probably won't go over well with your spouse.) Do this by clicking and treating your dog for taking the letter or newspaper and holding it without mouthing it.

2. Take a step or two away and have her bring it to you. Click and treat the motion of moving toward you.

3. Put the letter on the floor and tell your dog to Take It. You may want to use junk mail until your dog refines her techniques in picking up something so close to the floor.

4. When your dog is retrieving with finesse, begin to work her with the real mail pile or newspaper.

🐾 OH, YOU LITTLE SHOWOFF!

We all have a little showoff in us, and dogs are no exception. Dogs love to make us laugh and their antics often cheer us and relieve the stresses of everyday life. Taking the time to work with your dog will strengthen your bond with her and fine-tune your ability to communicate with each other. Your dog will love strutting her stuff.

Some dogs, because of their breeds or their personalities, just seem to be suited to elegant tricks. That's why it's so important to know your dog and understand him—so you can train him to his best advantage.

Hi-Ho Silver, Away!

This trick is a great way to show off a dog that likes to jump up on you. The only difference is your dog is not making physical contact with you when she is holding the rearing-horse position with her front legs stretched upward. The shaping steps for teaching Hi-Ho Silver, Away! are as follows:

1. Hold your hand as a target above your dog's head and click and treat her for touching it.
2. Gradually raise your hand until she is all the way up on her hind legs.
3. Practice frequently to help her build up her leg muscles.

4. Get your dog to hold the position by delaying the click and treat for several seconds.

5. Increase the time by a few seconds until she can hold the position for about fifteen seconds.

6. Cue your dog to extend her paws by using the Paw It command with your hand as a target.

7. Only click and treat versions of this behavior that are of longer duration and the correct position (front paws extended).

8. Fade the hand target by using it to start the behavior and then pulling it away. Click and treat your dog for continuing to perform the behavior in the absence of the target.

9. Replace the old cue with the new cue Away by saying the new cue right before the dog starts the behavior.

Sit Up Pretty

For this trick the dog is sitting on his hind legs with his front paws tucked into his chest. This is also a behavior that the dog needs to practice frequently to be able to build up his back and hind-end muscles. The shaping steps for teaching Sit Up Pretty are as follows:

1. Use your hand as a target and click and treat him for touching your hand while raising his front end off the ground.

2. Withhold the click and treat by a few seconds to get your dog to hold the position high enough to have him sitting up on his back end, but not standing.

3. Add a cue like Sit Up or Beg, by saying it right before the Touch cue.
4. The click and treat should happen as soon as the dog starts the behavior on the new cue.

Balance a Cookie on Your Nose

This trick demonstrates your dog's will power, because she must balance a cookie on her nose and wait to take the cookie until you say so.

1. Start with your dog in a Sit in front of you and click and treat her for staying.
2. Practice holding her muzzle and placing a cookie on her nose for a click and treat.
3. Repeat this last step until the dog can hold still for several seconds.
4. Slowly let go of your dog's muzzle and click and treat her for holding it steady.
5. Gradually increase the amount of time your dog balances the cookie on her nose before you click and treat.
6. You will probably find after a bit of practice that your dog develops a flip-and-catch technique to eat the cookie. This makes the trick all the more flashy and impressive.

🐾 HUMBLE DOG TRICKS

Although some dogs are prone to fancier tricks, others are, by nature, more sedate. These simple and adorable tricks suit their personalities, and will therefore be easier for you to teach. How you use the tricks, such as Say You're Sorry, is entirely up to you.

Say You're Sorry

For this trick the dog lies down with his chin on the ground between his front paws. An added bonus is teaching him to look up at you, which will add an even more convincing element to the performance. You may want to use this as the canine version of Time Out.

1. Put your dog in a Down, facing you; click and treat him for holding that position.
2. After about thirty seconds, withhold the click and wait. Pay close attention and click and treat any head motion down.
3. Once your dog starts to understand that lowering his head is what causes the click, withhold the click until your dog holds the position for an extra second.
4. Increase the seconds your dog has to keep his head down until you can build it up to fifteen to twenty seconds.
5. Label the behavior Sorry by saying the command right before he offers the behavior.
6. Repeat this step until the command Sorry triggers the behavior.

Say Your Prayers

Whether they are praying for leniency after getting into the garbage or praying for mud to roll in, any dog looks cute performing this trick. This trick requires your dog to rest her paws on a chair or stool and tuck her head between her front paws. She can be sitting or standing when she does this.

1. Use a table, stool, or chair that won't move when your dog puts her paws on it.
2. Get your dog to put her front paws on the stool by tapping the stool or luring her with a treat. Click any effort to get her paws up on the stool.
3. Delay the click so that your dog is putting her paws up and leaving them there for three seconds before you click and treat.
4. Using a yogurt lid as a target, get your dog to put her head between her front paws by placing the target slightly under her chest. Click and treat your dog for making attempts to touch the target.
5. Delay the click again until your dog holds her nose to the target for longer periods of time.
6. Fade the target slowly by clicking before she actually touches it, or by making it smaller.
7. Label the behavior Say Your Prayers as she is performing the behavior and just before any other cues. Gradually fade any old cues.

Go Get Mom

This can be a useful trick for kids and parents alike; for this trick the dog must go to a family member and lead them back to the person that sent them. This can be a great way to round up the family for dinnertime by sending the dog to bring each member to the table.

1. Using the person your dog is going to get as your helper, call the dog back and forth between you and click and treat him for going to each person.
2. When your dog is doing this enthusiastically, label the behavior Go and the person's name right before the person calls the dog to Come.
3. Move the people further apart so that the dog is going to the person from different rooms and up and down the stairs.
4. Replace the Come command with Go by saying Go Get Mom right before Mom calls the dog to come. The person the dog is searching for should be doing the clicking and treating when the dog finds them.
5. Once the dog starts to offer the behavior readily, he can be weaned off the clicker and treats, but he should still be acknowledged with praise and affection.

🐾 SUPERSMART TRICKS

You learned earlier that dogs can be trained to perform any task that they are physically capable of doing. That said, the critical factor to successfully performing these tricks is your patience in handling your dog. Start training your dog for these actions when you see that she is ready.

Ring a Bell

This trick involves teaching your dog to ring a bell with her nose or a paw. This trick is also quite practical, as you can teach your dog to ring a bell when she wants to go outside to the bathroom.

Hang a set of bells next to the door that you use to let your dog outside. Once she learns how to ring the bell with her mouth or nose, start having her do this each time she goes out to go potty. Pretty soon your dog will ring the bell to let you know she wants to go out. You may want to use a set of sleigh bells for this trick; four or five bells on a long strap make it easier for your dog to learn to ring a bell, because it will give her more opportunities to be right. The shaping steps for teaching your dog to Ring a Bell are as follows:

1. Put the bells on the floor and click and treat your dog for sniffing them (you can use a Touch command if she knows one).
2. Delay the click and wait for her to touch harder or mouth them before you click and treat.
3. Work at this until she's ringing the bells with purpose.
4. Hang the bells next to the door and repeat the above steps until she is ringing them reliably.
5. Gradually increase the distance she must travel to touch the bells.
6. Verbally label ringing the bells, Bells.

Dancing Dog

This trick is adorable but difficult for most dogs. To perform this trick the dog must balance on his hind legs and walk. You'll want to practice in short sessions to help your dog build up his back and leg muscles gradually. Be sure to work on a nonskid surface so that your dog does not injure himself. The shaping steps for teaching Dancing Dog are as follows:

1. With your dog in a Sit, hold your hand slightly above his nose and click and treat any effort to raise himself up on his back legs to touch your hand.
2. Raise your hand higher and continue to click and treat your dog for using his hind end to raise himself up and touch your hand.
3. Get your dog to hold the position longer by delaying the click by a second or two.
4. Gradually increase the time to several seconds.
5. Move your hand around and click and treat him for walking on his hind legs to touch it.
6. Turn your hand in a circle and click and treat your dog for walking on his hind legs to follow it.
7. Add the cue Dance by saying it just before the dog starts the behavior.

Enjoy spending time teaching your dog tricks and performing them for friends and family. Developing a healthy training relationship with your dog will make it easier to communicate with her and help you to gain control of behavior problems. Besides, every soldier needs to have some fun!

Resources

Books

Burch, Mary R. and Jon S. Bailey. *How Dogs Learn* (Hungry Minds, Inc.).

Campbell, William E. *Behavior Problems in Dogs*, Third Revised Edition (BehaviorRx Systems).

Cantrell, Krista. *Catch Your Dog Doing Something Right: How to Train Any Dog in Five Minutes a Day* (Plume Publishers).

Donaldson, Jean. *The Culture Clash* (James and Kenneth Publishing).

Donaldson, Jean. *Dogs Are from Neptune* (Lasar Multimedia Productions).

Dunbar, Ian. *Dr. Dunbar's Good Little Dog Book* (James and Kenneth Publisher).

———. *How to Teach a New Dog Old Tricks* (James and Kenneth Publishing).

Owens, Paul. *The Dog Whisperer, 2nd Edition: A Compassionate, Nonviolent Approach to Dog Training* (Adams Media).

Pryor, Karen. *Don't Shoot the Dog: The New Art of Teaching and Training*, Revised Edition (Bantam Books).

Rugaas, Turid. *On Talking Terms with Dogs: Calming Signals* (Legacy By Mail).

Ryan, Terry. *The Toolbox for Remodeling Your Problem Dog* (Howell Book House).

Tellington-Jones, Linda. *Getting in Touch with Your Dog: A Gentle Approach to Influencing Health, Behavior, and Performance* (Trafalgar Square).

Wilkes, Gary. *A Behavior Sampler* (Sunshine Books).

Organizations

The Association of Pet Dog Trainers (APDT)
Phone: 800-738-3647
Web site: *www.apdt.com*
Search the database for a list of trainers in your area.

Delta Society
Phone: 425-226-7357
Web site: *www.deltasociety.org*
E-mail: *info@deltasociety.org*

Therapy Dogs International
E-mail: *tdi@gti.net*

Whole-Dog-Journal.com
Phone: 800-829-9165
Web site: *www.whole-dog-journal.com*
A monthly guide to natural dog care and training.

Web Sites

Association of Pet Dog Trainers (APDT): *www.apdt.com*

Canine University®: *www.canineuniversity.com*

Karen Pryor's Clicker Training Site: *www.clickertraining.com*

DogWise: *www.dogwise.com*

Index